I0582356

REMEMBERING THE ALCHEMISTS

& Other Essays

Richard Hoffman

THE Press

2023

REMEMBERING THE ALCHEMISTS
& Other Essays

Printed in the United States of America

First Edition

ISBN-13: 978-1-7345177-6-7 (pbk)

Hoffman, Richard 1949 —

Remembering The Alchemists & Other Essays

1. Essay 2. Memoir 3. History 4. Poetry

10 9 8 7 6 5 4 3 2 1

Front cover art by William Blake — "Cain Fleeing from the Wrath of God (The Body of Abel Found by Adam and Eve)," watercolor, black ink, and graphite on cream wove paper. Courtesy of Harvard Art Museums/Fogg Museum, Bequest of Grenville L. Winthrop, Photo ©President and Fellows of Harvard College, 1943.401

Back cover art by William Blake — "Then a Spirit Passed Before My Face (The Book of Job)," engraving. Courtesy of Harvard Art Museums/Fogg Museum, Bequest of Grenville L. Winthrop, Photo ©President and Fellows of Harvard College, 1943.412

for Damion, Emory, Savannah,
Nicholas, and Olivia

and, as always, for Kathi

REMEMBERING THE ALCHEMISTS

& Other Essays

Also by Richard Hoffman:

Half the House

Without Paradise

Gold Star Road

Interference & Other Stories

Emblem

Love & Fury

Noon until Night

Contents

LIKE NEVER BEFORE

> "If the spectator could enter into these images in his imagination, ...could make a friend and companion of one of these images of wonder... then would he arise from his grave, then would he meet the Lord in the air, and then he would be happy."
>
> — Blake

I'D BEEN READING Leo Damrosch's insightful and inspiriting *Eternity's Sunrise: The Imaginative World of William Blake* and was praising it to my friend Richard, also a writer. He mentioned that the Harvard Museums had a number of Blake's watercolors and etchings and that we could request to see anything in the museum's holdings, so we selected eight pieces from their online catalogue, some from *The Divine Comedy*, others from *The Book of Job*, along with the "Frontispiece" to *America: A Prophecy,* and made an appointment.

We were met by a cordial member of the curatorial staff and escorted to a viewing room, where the works were propped, unmatted, on reading stands on both sides of a table, four to a side. I had expected to view them under glass, I suppose, or arrayed in a display case, but here they were, and their vulnerability seemed shocking: watercolor and ink on paper, by Blake's own hand. I felt reverent.

I ambled around the table, stopping first to view "Then a Spirit Passed Before My Face" from Blake's illustrations for *The Book of Job,* its alternate title, "The Vision of Eliphaz" identifying its main figure.

In the painting, Eliphaz, one of Job's neighbors, is recounting a nightmare, and as I stared at it I began to think of it as a brilliant explication of the magic of storytelling. Eliphaz is seated on the ground with Job and his wife and the other two friends, Bildad and Zophar, who have come to try to comfort Job, a mission they botch magnificently. As Eliphaz tells his story, his arm is raised toward a kind of thought balloon that takes up the top two thirds of the painting. All the others (including us, viewing the painting) follow his arm's cue and look not at him but at the represented story he tells, which hovers over them all. He is not looking up, however, he is looking at his listeners looking up. He knows he's got them, they are in his thrall. In the cloud of story over them, Eliphaz is in his bed, confronted by a figure terrifying enough to make his hair stand on end. (And what is more terrifying than a nightmare that takes place in your own bedroom, in which dream and waking realities share the same frame?) Excited but not wanting to disturb my friend's viewing across the table, I made a note to come back to this painting and talk about it with him, eager to tell him what I thought I saw in it, the commentary on imagination, on dream, on storytelling as performance and manipulation.

The colors of the "Frontispiece for *America: A Prophecy"* seemed to have faded. The copy on display was a bit murky and I didn't spend much time with it. But when I glimpsed the painting, "Cain Fleeing from the Wrath of God" or "The Body of Abel Found by Adam and Eve," I veered, nearly without volition, from my orderly circuit of the displayed works, and sat before it. It is a small watercolor, but into it Blake has compressed not only a tremendous understanding of the human tragedy, but also the essence of his artistic ambitions. In the Descriptive Catalogue to his Exhibition of 1809, held at James Blake's shop in Broad Street, Golden Square, London, Blake wrote that it is one of the drawings that "...the Artist wishes were in Fresco on an enlarged scale to ornament the altars of Churches, and to make England, like Italy, respected by respectable men of other countries on account of Art."

The painting is shocking, especially among the works we had chosen. Here, unlike the ethereal blues and grays of the other selected pieces, the colors are garish, loud, uncouth, the palette in keeping with the content, and the tableaux is all movement and imbalance. The colors and composition made sense to me, as if the painting were saying that there can be no harmony after the crime depicted here, and on the heels of that thought came the realization that the very first death, at least in terms of our mythic understanding, was a murder, a fratricide! Despite its small size, the painting seemed equal to the enormity of that understanding, and I sat there reverberating with it. The sun is eclipsed by streaks of dark clouds. It is literally appalling. And the impossible happens now. Fire, not water, falls from the sky. Everything is wrong.

I was transfixed and astonished. I couldn't move. The lesser awe I had been feeling before the other works — mostly that I was in such intimate contact with them, with these one-of-a-kind, original, hand-made images — gave way to something else, something more intense and profound that I couldn't and still don't fully understand. I only know that the image, the entire composition, was seared into my mind so that for several nights afterward I couldn't sleep. If it were music we would call it an earworm. It would not depart. Unlike music it was not a loop in time but a continual full-on confrontation, as if the image were forever hurtling toward me, bearing down on me. And like an earworm, to note the occasional respite from it, even gratefully, was to activate it once again.

Cain is stepping out of the grave he had been digging to bury his brother. There is a shovel lying on the ground. There is anguish and horror on his face and he grips his own skull as if to tear it apart. *How could I have done this? How could I have thought I might hide it and therefore forget it? Forget my own brother? What manner of monster am I?*

Here, in the figure of Cain, the discovery of the knowledge of good and evil is honed to a bitter sharpness, the knowledge so much more painful than any could have supposed: *I am, myself, the agent of evil. I am, myself, the foulness I had feared.*

I took up the magnifying glass I'd been provided, but I found I could not bear to look too closely or too long at Cain's face. The horror there awakened a terror I was loathe to feel.

Looking from the figure of Cain in flight, the fire of his guilt singeing him as he pivots from the grave, to the figures on the right side of the composition, the painting's alternate title, "The Body of Abel Found by Adam and Eve" becomes a more apt description of the scene. In a kind of knot from which Cain will now forever be excluded, on the other side of the unfinished grave, are Adam, Eve, and Abel. Eve bends over Abel's body, seems to collapse over him, her hair cascading across his corpse in a torrent of the purest grief. We can't see her face. She is hidden in her agony, and perhaps in her awful self-recrimination as well: her memories of paradise, yes, but also her act, her choice, the antecedent to this tragedy. She who only recently became aware of sequence now encounters consequence.

Adam is stunned, astonished, a rictus of terror, stuck in a moment that will never end, ineffectual, wronged and wrong, paralytic, twisted, broken. He is unique among men because he cannot look to history for a reason for this horror, either to make excuses or to try, for the sake of the future, to understand. It could be that what we call history, and the seeking to find some meaning in it, both begin in this moment. So much begins in this moment, with Abel lying on the hard ground, his head back, his beardless young chin tilted toward the sky.

Adam's dumbstruck face says that he gets it now, not only what it means to be outside of paradise, but here, on earth, in time. And it is not the sudden fact of death that has undone him — although undone he is, the last vestiges of any paradisal naïveté are gone from him now — so much as this presence of evil, of fatal discord, of the impossibility, ever again, of peace. His body, still Edenic, perfect, muscled and symmetrical, is in a kind of spasm, depicted in the exact moment of his revelation, every muscle seized, contracted, with his hands turned up at the wrists, bent back as far as they can go, his fingers spread as far as they can go toward a full expression of his shock. His mouth is open but it's clear no sound is coming out, no cry, and certainly no words. Eve, however, is wailing. We know this. We cannot see her face, but her posture, bent over the body of her child, her voluminous hair cascading over Abel's shoulders, is the posture of weeping and we know that kind of weeping, that awful sound.

Perhaps Adam will join Eve later in the bodily expression of grief, the sobbing, the moaning and keening. For both of them, language, whatever language we imagine them speaking, is absent, unavailable. Might language return, changed by this? Might it return after Abel's body, laid out next to this grave that Cain has dug, is rolled into the earth and covered?

And so, Cain becomes the archetype of the person who discovers, with horror, the evil he has done in passion, and its meaning, and therefore his impossible responsibility: to know himself capable of inflicting death. That not only is the world this bloody place, and not a peaceable kingdom where trees bear fruit and crops in orderly rows are nurtured by sun and rain, but that he himself is the agent of that revelation.

Consider Adam's complete uselessness; consider that for him as a father understanding this uselessness is nothing less than psychic annihilation. He is as empty as a zero. His face and posture suggest authority completely at a loss, shocked, outraged, and completely bewildered by the indelible fact that his son is dead — at the hands of his son. Patriarchy, the painting might suggest, is a lie, a pathetic insistence upon an authority that here, in this scene, has been revealed as hollow: Adam, no man's son, is the defeated father; from now on, sons will hand down to their sons contention, aggression, violence, in a future that is martial, bloody, and murderous. The look on the face of Blake's Adam suggests he sees and understands this all at once.

Abel's body is everyone else, all our bodies, the spectre of our fear at being vulnerable to deadly violence.

The scene depicts a moment when even the dream of a return to paradise has become impossible. If there is an angel standing guard at the gate, he has extinguished his now superfluous flaming sword: Eden is gone for good. This is the moment when Adam and Eve, in their wordlessness and wailing, in their grief, become the parents of the human race.

2

> "You are the maker of the dream … Whatever you put into the dream must be what is in you."
>
> — Fritz Perls

I am a shovel of iron and wood. I do not recall being made although it's likely I am Cain's creation, he who makes his own ingenious tools, who gathers seeds and plants in rows, who in the past has used me to prepare a harvest. Together we made an orchard of a wilderness. A garden from the stories of his parents. I am burnished by his hands. I smell of him, his labor. I believe he loves me. I will do anything he asks.

I felt the desperate yearning in his hands, in the rhythm of his work as together we opened the ground. And so I must believe he only wished to see his brother again. Other dead things have all come back, placed in the earth and covered, why not Abel? Though I sensed he knew before he threw me aside that he was lying to himself with every chunk of sod we broke, with every shovelful of dirt.

I was not his weapon, only his accomplice. He will flee and leave me here, abandoned. I think this is the edge of a cliff. I sense it. With my metal I can smell the coming rain. It will douse the flames, but Cain will be gone from here.

Who then will bury Abel who is not a seed and will not come again? I await them.

We mountains are all that does not aspire, does not contend. Grey, barren, craggy, forbidding, we seem to go on forever and we are pleased to have you think so. Hidden in our rock are jewels and geodes, veins of silver and gold; in our caves there are dangerous hungers. Look in every direction, look as far as your eyes can see: nothing grows here. A little moss on a hollow filled with dirt, a solitary bowl of earth Cain must have had to search for, a little stage on which to play the human tragedy. Let the wind and rain continue sculpting us. Let every path lead to a precipice. We care nothing for your puny awe.

The book says I am flint but I know nothing of that. As far as I am concerned that book is far in the future; besides, I don't need a description of myself. I am not only dead, I have always been dead. I was the first to welcome Abel to Sheol, as the book calls it. His blood is upon me, quite literally. Still, I cannot be held responsible. I am only a broken piece of the former world. I can enkindle but I do not burn. I don't care what they say, Richard, William, Cain— and you, yes, you — I am not you. Nor could I ever wish to be. Now for Ables' sake, who is my brother now, no longer yours — get these words off of me!

I will find my way to the center of the earth. It calls to me, would drink me. Until I find my way there, it is decreed I cannot rest. All my lineage, through which I would have otherwise flowed, cry out from the ground.

3

In the biblical account, God places a mark on Cain to defend him from the wrath of others, but who these others are is unexplained: until this moment there have been no other people in the narrative, no one outside its frame. Cain seems violently twisted, seen in flight from the disrupted order, from the half finished grave, from the rest of his family. Some accounts have God putting a curse on Cain after his attempt to hide, so that, forever after, he is marked as one with a different fate, one who is easily seen to be "other," perhaps by the haunted look in his eyes, by the evidence of trauma he carries with him.

The body hides nothing from the bodies of others, even if we have learned, of necessity or politeness or fear, not to acknowledge what our bodies perceive.

From one perspective it is the body that is ageless, deathless, reconstituted generation after generation, an uninterrupted generative eternity, while the self is a contingent and grievously temporary complex of language and experience and circumstance.

A self must learn. The body is. The body knows. A self learns to act as if it is real, and learns to ignore what the body knows. The body transcends the self and not, as religions have it, the other way round; even when they posit a stand-in for the self called the soul, the idea is that a personal transcendence is possible and ought to be sought after. Begin with that orientation to the divine, and one can talk all one wants about charity, generosity, brotherhood — it's every man for himself. Even before there were religions there was religious war.

Cain's turn is away from all that existed before his rage overtook him. But what is it exactly that he flees, that he turns from so violently? Those flames are driving him from the anguish of his mother, wheeling him away from the sudden sense of himself as monstrous, an understanding he derives from his father's horrified countenance.

Everything that will ever be will be *after* this flight. Cain is also banished from the pale and compensating paradise of familiarity, forever comfortless. Perhaps his anxiety, his discontent, his jittery manner, his bitten nails, his occasional outbursts of defiant anger are the marks by which he will be known, a warning to others that before engaging with him it is necessary to grasp that he inhabits a nightmare.

It is a nightmare for which he believes he is solely responsible. But is he? In the story, the smoke from his sacrifice turns downward. It must have stung his eyes, burned his throat, set him coughing before it left him feeling rejected, disfavored, and abused. His subsequent confrontation with his brother marks, then, the further unfolding of a story that the Lord of the garden could only have written in a vindictive rage of his own. And it is the further expression of that vengeful and fiery animosity that he flees now, fully believing himself a monster.

His flight, as depicted by Blake, is also from the grave he has dug for his brother, from his attempt to hide the body of Abel. The nightmare he must live now is memory, history. The earth, the painting suggests, is hard, unaccommodating. Digging that grave must have been backbreaking labor. (Speaking figuratively —and of course we are, here, and have been all along, speaking figuratively — the digging must have taken a long, long time.) When Abel is at last placed in that hole, what then? Does the grave become a scar? A numb place where a brother had been? An ache that will turn Cain's attention away, from time to time, from the requirements of his troubled life?

How many times must Cain relive this moment before he can learn to abide? How many times will he throw down the shovel, leave his work, take flight from the uncomprehending faces of his loved ones? "After such knowledge, what forgiveness?" The darkness gathering, the shadows of the mountains moving and sliding over one another, the rumbling of thunder — can this nightmare, repeated forever, be his fate? In what direction might he turn to wake? It is one thing to be marked by trauma, another to be defined by it.

Oh, Cain, my brother, I would tackle you if I could; I would throw my body at yours, head first, and drive my shoulder into your thigh above the knee so your own weight would take you down. I would tackle you as I would tackle a burning child and try to dowse the fire, to cover you and smother the flames.

I have fled my own actions in horror. I have feared my own mind. I have cried out in my sudden understanding of my nature. I know.

You will attempt to forget. For a time the prospect of that forgetting, while you are digging the grave into which you will consign what you cannot bear, will provide relief.

But then the voice. Just as you are about to carry out the burial, that voice of fire.

Blake's painting is an illumination of the nightmarish vision of a storyteller who is removed from the story. Unlike the "Vision of Eliphaz" Blake includes no frame around this fearful dream. There is no before or after except for the implied parentheses around this moment. The painting itself leaves an indelible mark; it has left such a mark on me. It is an image from which I want to — but cannot — flee.

4

Many scholars have remarked that there are words missing from the text, that there seems to be a missing verse in the story. I bring this up here at the risk of sounding like one of those TV voice-overs promising *Biblical Mysteries Revealed!* — "Could it be that this missing verse holds the key to the future of mankind?" But it's true that many manuscripts, throughout centuries of copying, acknowledge this idea by leaving a space there.

Most English versions of the tale, derived from Greek translations, read, "And Cain spoke to his brother Abel." The Hebrew original, however, translated more accurately, reads "And Cain said to Abel, his brother," — but not, strangely, *what* he said.

One could read the missing words as a Biblical "meta" communication, an instance of narrative aphasia like a hole in the paper, a smudge, an ellipsis, in which the counterfactual is contained as well as the unknown: not only do we not know what transpired between these two characters, but the silence, the blankness, the failure of that exchange, represents the portal to an alternate history, a life on earth shaped differently, a tale that now can never be told, a version only glimpsed via yearning. Otherwise we might be celebrating the story as the first and foundational instance of successful diplomacy, and not the birth of the mute fratricidal rage we know as history.

In fact, in that gap, in those absent words, is the absence of language itself. Had Cain been able to speak of his envy and how it made him suffer, he might well have found, with his brother, the first real peace, not merely the absence of conflict, but its resolution, which here, now, far from paradise, is a thing much more to be desired.

Of the many things the painting stirs in me, including fear and sadness, is the vain hope that we can right ourselves, that understanding our own nature can save us, that although we cannot know eternity while we remain adrift in time, it is not too late. As Seamus Heaney has put it, "If you have the words, there's always a chance that you'll find the way." It is a poet's dutiful faith, that when world and word match up we are back, if only for moment, in the garden. But we also know, and seem to have always known, that when we fail to find the words, we murder.

Inside the Nabi Habeel Mosque outside Damascus is a sarcophagus twenty-three feet long, draped with green silk on which are verses from the Qur'an. It seems to have survived, so far, the political violence in Syria that has damaged or destroyed so many other shrines. Islamic tradition has it that Abel is buried there, and the local people seem willing to believe that, along with the rest of his family, he was nearly that tall. No doubt if one were to argue that nowhere on earth have human bones of such length ever been found, one would be viewed as an ignoramus for not acknowledging and accepting that we are in the realm of the imagination, where the suspension of disbelief is the beginning of spiritual understanding. It is a fiction, an invitation, a prompt, a sacred region of consciousness reserved for poetry. Our forebears were giants.

Similarly, a change of perspective is required to grasp the intimate immensity of time, to appreciate that Abel's corpse exists in eternity because nothing ever vanishes. Even modern science would concur: what exists eventually becomes unrecognizable but it never wholly ceases, and certainly our pedestrian view of time as an arrow from birth to death is mistaken, as wrong as a literal belief in the movement of the sun across the sky, both products of our limited perspective.

And so, Blake's painting: The ephemerality of the event here succumbs not only to *ars longa,* but to its reverberating and compounding consequences, meaning that the entire drama continues to exist and ramify, and therefore our response to it must be, can only be, in the present. The painting remains an illumination of present reality, not merely the illustration of an old story.

According to the Vietnamese Buddhist Master Thich Nhat Hanh. "When we're able to embrace our suffering, we're also embracing our ancestors, and the healing goes back through the generations." According to the writer Marilyn Robinson, this was also the view of Puritan Divine, Jonathan Edwards, "there should be two judgments: one when we die, and one when the full impact of our lives has played itself out." In other words, the meaning of an event can be changed after the fact by action in the present to change "the full impact" even of historical crimes.

Look again at Cain's face! Look at his eyes: what he sees is not what is in front of him but what is behind: Abel's grave, Abel's body, and his parents, from whom he is fleeing as surely as from God, no matter what the title of the painting says. He is a human comet, hurtling toward us, his descendants.

Human nature, its interplay of memory and genetics and culture, seems to be an endless and inexorable cascade of violence. And while poetry, defined as language meant to describe, contain, understand, and mitigate that destiny, an oceanic reservoir of possible concord, seems the only way out, there is, in fact, no such place as "out."

And so, where does that leave us after millennia of carnage, horror and grief? Either you believe in the sanctity of an individual human life without exception, or you believe that some people are expendable and deserve to lie on the earth without moving while those who love them wail and moan over them. If we are thereby descendants of Cain, we are worse, much worse, than he, because we have made ourselves a world in which our a priori rationalizations relieve us of the horror and shame of our murders. Worse, we call that exculpatory arrangement civilization.

I feel sure that just as Adam's open mouth emits no sound whatever, Cain is howling, a roar from his broad chest, and that the echo of this event is history. If there were any of us outside the nightmare, any of us outside the frame, if there ever could be, we would only perceive a disquiet, a stirring in sleep, a muffled cry, a whimper. After all, the rest of nature seems undisturbed; the stars crowd the heavens and animals call to one another in the night outside. Would that it were so easy, that we could take history by the shoulder and give it a squeeze: *Cain, Cain, wake up, you're dreaming.*

BEWILDERED PASSENGERS

ALTHOUGH NO ADULTS had declared it off-limits, the trainyard gave off the creosote smell of the forbidden. The place felt dangerous, with grass tall as our thighs, insects buzzing, grasshoppers springing this way and that in the brittle summer heat. It was the kind of place where I always seemed to end up with Patrick. My mother loved it whenever he rang the doorbell because she'd likely been trying to get me to put down my book and go outside. "You're going to hurt your eyes with your nose always stuck in a book like that." If she only knew the kinds of places we went: to the swamp behind the dairy, the cliffs above the quarry, the razor-wired scrap yard with the chained twin Dobermans.

One rusted railroad track split into two there, and a huge vertical lever that would send the train down one track or the other jutted up from a rusty stanchion deep in the weeds by the footpath that Patrick and I had followed half a mile to get there. Neither of us was strong enough to budge it, although we tried, first each of us alone — competitively, as if trying to pull Excalibur from the stone — then joining forces, the combined 150 pounds of us grunting and straining. Nothing doing. Patrick spit. A thumb-sized grasshopper landed on my sneaker and I kicked him off.

That's when I started wondering what would have happened if we had managed, with all our 12-year-old might, to screech the rusty inner track those few impossible inches. Where might the train have arrived? I pictured people disembarking in a busy city — New York to the east, Chicago to the west — some of them laughing and shaking their heads, some puzzled and asking one another what happened, some irate at the conductor.

And what if we had put the train on a collision course? What if miles from here, a desperate horn blew just before the terrible wreck, cars buckled and broken, uncoupled, overturned, dead bodies everywhere and all because of us?

We hadn't considered any of it, testing ourselves against the intractable adult world; not for a single moment. I thought I understood something about us then. I looked at Patrick who had begun throwing rocks, trying to land them in a freight wagon. All around us were freight cars and open wagons and flatbeds, and it dawned on me that none of them had moved in months, maybe years.

Patrick lobbed a big rock into a rusty gondola. "Let's go home," he said. "This is boring."

AN EGG

DARESN'T. I WOKE to the word. I heard it, just that single word, trailing a waning echo for a long time, like a fading bell. I have only ever heard two people use that word, my mother and my grandmother, both dead for decades, both intoning it with index finger raised. I'd been asleep for nearly twelve hours, hiding. That's what I do now during times I can't go on, those times when grief and sadness come visiting unannounced, when — no matter the love and laughter of the present — the past, unfinished, requires its tribute. I used to drink myself into oblivion whenever those times came round, until I came to prefer oblivion to living and so drank all the time. These days, when it gets too bad, I just sleep.

A contraction for dares not, used with no concern for person or number. Always an imperative or admonition, the raised index marking a boundary. I daresn't; you daresn't; he, she, or it daresn't; we daresn't; youse daresn't; they daresn't. You daresn't think that, say that, do that.

I can't pinpoint where this sadness comes from. I suspect it's a piling up of things, of many different sadnesses. Mostly it is the sorrow of losing two brothers to a wasting and fatal illness that filled our home with sadness and sighing and a grim resolve, a sorrow I seem never to have been able to shake.

It is the sadness of watching my parents' once joyful marriage worn to their dutiful and bickering years-long deathwatch over my brothers, and their utter exhaustion afterward. It is the trauma of a sexual assault in boyhood that from time to time returns as a panicked confusion or sudden aphasia.

I thought that all I had to do was remain sober, and for thirty years that sufficed, more or less. I didn't drink, didn't do drugs, quit smoking, learned to take care of myself. But some days I still find myself overwhelmed, unable to get out of my bed. It could be argued that that's an improvement on getting hammered or wasted, or that I am simply a person who needs a lot of sleep, who rises much later than my wife, up with the sun each morning. But I recognize it as the same old oblivion-seeking, the same need for escape. I'm just so good at it now that I don't need chemical assistance.

I understood the admonition: I daresn't despair. Because that's the step I was about to take, led there following self-pity's downward path; right there, where the emptiness begins, I lay curled like a fetus. Another long night of no dreams, another long night of no dreams I could remember, until that voice, and that one word: *daresn't.*

I know who it was who spoke to me. I know to whom I am grateful.

But why are nearly all my memories of my mother from before the age of six or seven? Are those even memories in the same way other episodes from my childhood can be summoned, plotted on a time-line, and understood, more or less, in relation to other events? My first playground fight, when a kid from the Washington School dumped all my schoolwork out of my bag and tore it in pieces — my bloody nose, my broken hand; first kiss, in Mary Ellen Moffett's backyard, sitting on the bulkhead to the root cellar, smell of fallen apples and the hum of bees; friendships, betrayals, the terrible remorse in the dark confessional, the proud report-cards, making the teams, winning and losing, striking a pose and finding a persona that no one would laugh at, the first few blonde and silky whiskers: all that masculine romance of growing up, all that imagination I call memory encoded somehow as sticky stuff in the seams of my convoluted brain.

I was uptown with my mother. I remember a trolley car, which makes this a very early memory because I was born in 1949, and the last trolley on Hamilton Street ceased carrying passengers to the offices and department stores up and down that wide boulevard in 1952. I believe this is my very first memory, this one bright noisy moment of screeches and sparks and ringing bells that somehow made it through my toddler's trance to become not only the first of my memories, but the beginning of memory itself, what I have from time to time, carelessly, called my life, and which I now just call my story.

Falling sparks! Blue and buzzing. And white sparks shooting out from screeching metal wheels, and people getting on and off, unconcerned by fear or wonder. And amid the shrieking of wheels on steel, a bell: *dingding dingding*. And the gray and blue behemoth shudders and lurches forward into a day in winter — yes, I remember snow — when I was three.

We may have gone uptown to pay the electric bill because another incident I associate with that day is a sickening vertigo when looking up at the towering Pennsylvania Power & Light building. I looked up, and up, and up, through the falling snow, until my stomach flipped and I became dizzy and I thought the angels were pulling me up to heaven but I didn't want to go. I know this because my mother once told me that right before I fainted, falling to the sidewalk and peeing my pants, I yelled, "No!"

But looking back, I think that after a certain age, seven or so, I was no longer a child but something else called a boy, which is a different creature entirely. Boys want to be big boys and big boys don't cry because they want to be men. After that unnoticed transition, the compromising embrace of that aspiration, I was my father's son, not my mother's child, and I can see that, in a way that pains me to admit, I lost her then. This understanding surfaced from deep in my grief when she died at the age of 56, just after my first child, a son, was born. Even now I remain angry at an arrangement — partly practical, accidental, and particular to my family's somewhat unique situation, but also largely social and political — that conscripted me into the world of men, a world where I was injured into a further ignorance of women useful to that arrangement.

Not only was that first fistfight a debacle, but I had to make up a story for my mother to account for it. I knew that I daresn't stop at The Washington School playground on the way home from St. Francis of Assisi School; it was strictly forbidden. Washington was a public school, its students presumably Protestant. There was entirely no ecumenical spirit in the neighborhoods in those days; in fact, the public and Catholic high schools no longer played football against each other because of the violence that surrounded the game. There had been smashed windshields, stabbings, even on one occasion gunshots.

It happened like this: I had put down my book bag to climb the monkey bars. We had nothing like them on the playground at St. Francis. In fact, there wasn't much of anything on the playground there; it was just a big parking lot we could use for our games of keep-away, freeze-tag, red light-green light. I was so involved with trying to overcome my fear of heights and with getting up the courage to try to hang upside down as I'd seen another kid do, knees hooked over the topmost bar, arms folded across his chest, seeming to approve of the upside down world, that I didn't notice my bag was gone until I'd climbed back down.

A torn paper blew past me in the wind; others skittered along the ground or stuck to the chainlink fence: my homework! Pages from my schoolbooks! On top of a fencepost, my book bag, now empty, hanging above my reach.

"Hey! Francis-the-sissy! Whatcha crying for, Francis-the-sissy?" Kids from The Washington School converged on me. One pushed me, then another, until I pushed back at one of them. "Fight! Fight! Fight! Fight!" they chanted rhythmically and made a circle. I seemed to have chosen my opponent, the one I pushed back, who took a boxing stance and was sizing me up. We were ringed by chanting boys and there was no way out.

It was over quickly, and I had broken my right hand. It is the only thing I recall of the whole fight and it still makes me wince: my opponent ducking so the first real punch I'd thrown in my young life landed not on his cheek where I'd aimed it but on the crown of his head. My pinky was jammed up into my hand, the skin at its base crumpled, pleated as a concertina. I tried to fend off my attacker with my left, but I was down in the dirt and knew enough to stay down.

The pain in my hand didn't start until I was walking home with my empty book bag; by the time I got there, with a bloody lip and a mouse above one eye, I was howling and my hand was starting to resemble an oven mitt.

What sort of a *being* was she, my mother? Not only what sort of person, but preceding even that elaboration — via time, culture, and circumstance — what sort of *being* was she? Adjectives: female, resilient, bouyant, libidinous, graceful, social, religious, down-to-earth. Writing this, I feel as if I am stalking my mother, trying to catch a glimpse of her, to see her from different angles — literally, through the windows of first our house on 9th Street, and then the house we moved to on 13th. I am a kind of voyeur, a spy from the future, although I don't know what I'm looking for, exactly, nor who I am to report to.

To ask who my mother would have been had my brothers not been afflicted with Duchenne Muscular Dystrophy, if her life had not been tightly circumscribed by their daily needs, is like trying to imagine what the world would be like in five dimensions, or if life were magnesium based, or the sun orbited the moon. Impossible, although I have tried.

What I daresn't do is forget her, even if I have to create her.

My brother Joe, the only other survivor of the six of us, sent me some photos he found of our mother. In both she seems happy; in one her head is thrown back in a way I remember that means she will recover in a moment with an exuberant riposte, or a joke of her own — *(How do you find an old man in the dark? It's not hard.)* In the other she is smiling attentively, anticipating further enjoyment. In that one, I can see my grandmother's arthritic hands, her crooked fingers, folded on the table next to an ashtray. The photos seem to underscore the message: you not only daresn't be defeated, daresn't quit, you have to retain the capacity for mirth, for playful vulgarity, for joy.

I mention to my brother that our mother was certainly resilient. "Oh yeah," he says, "somehow she never let anything get her down for more than a day or two, and then she was her smiling self again. At least that's how I remember her. I don't know how she did it. She certainly didn't get much help."

The lie I told my mother, as she yanked the lever and freed the ice-cubes from their tray, was a put-up job, an improvised bit of bricolage: I said I'd been side-swiped by a car. (A week earlier, the kid across the street had stepped out between two cars and got clipped. His name was Bobby, the same as my younger brother's. I was drawing or coloring at the kitchen table when we heard the terrible screech of brakes and the next moment someone shrieked, "Bobby!" My mother screamed and ran for the front door. My brother was sitting there on the steps as a crowd gathered across the street. "But Mom I stayed on the steps! I stayed on the steps!" he kept saying as she steered him inside.) The car had grazed me, I said, and sent my book bag sliding across the street where it hit the curb, spilling its contents down the storm sewer! I spun the story right out of the fear I'd seen on my mother's face the week before and even added grounds for outrage: the driver kept on going!

When my father got home, he first made believe he was examining my injury, "Hmm...I see...hmm..." then yanked the finger back out of my hand and into place before I even began to scream. He made a splint with a popsicle stick and black electrical tape from his toolbox. I don't think he bought the story my mother relayed to him. I don't recall if I had to tell the lie for a second time at school the next day; I suppose I must have but I can't say I remember.

It is an awesome power, the power to reshape the past. It could be that the awful estrangement that became so clear to me years later when my mother lay dying began with that first lie. And yet that fiction was, in some respects, a necessary separation from her, a kind of second birth. I was born again, baptized by the necessity to lie, and I have lived ever since among the fallen, here in the prevaricating world my mother left too soon, where telling, or sometimes even knowing, the truth remains perilous and perplexing and ever more difficult.

I wanted to hold onto the word. It had come to me in such a mysterious way, a matrilineal injunction from a dream, a warning but also an encouragement in the most literal sense of that word. I thought to print the word, large, and tack it on the wall of my study, or maybe even paint it on a small rock or something to keep in my pocket, like one of those tacky inspirational stones you buy in a gift shop. But the meaning of the word morphed, as words often do, and darkened when I thought of it in relation to my mother's life.

In the first half of the 20th century, when my mother came of age, she was directed and curtailed, modified and shaped, by descriptors. She left girlhood to become a dame, a broad, a skirt, a chick, a babe, a dish, a doll. Everyone agrees, and the grayscale photos show, that she was a beautiful young woman with a brilliant smile. And there was much she daresn't do.

When I say that my most powerful memories of my mother, and my strongest feelings for her, are rooted in my pre-school years, I don't mean to say that she was later absent from my life, or that my father was not also a presence during that time. Nor is it true that she is less a part of who I am. She is, however, harder to recall, to reimagine, than my father. One way or another, boyhood is a mercilessly gendered crucible of becoming, and in our family my mother was the only female. At the same time, I may find it so difficult to conjure her not because she is less but because she is more deeply a part of who I am. The Jesuits have a saying: "Give me the child to the age of seven, and I will give you the man." Here the gendered noun may be all the more true. And who was the most profound influence on me until about that age? My mother, hands down.

Of course there's another possibility: I never separated from her at all, not really; the evidence of such individuation would be some sort of adult relationship, and for complex reasons we never had that. The fact of my two brothers' affliction with Duchenne, their need for constant care; my "escape" to college in New York City; my need, in the aftermath of being raped by a coach at the age of ten, to hide my pain and confusion from her — all these forces created and widened our estrangement. I kept my sadness and confusion hidden with a cheery countenance, pecks on the cheek, hugs, the swapping of the "dirty jokes" she liked so much, and anything else I could come up with to reassure her that I was succeeding in becoming an adult.

But in those early years, when I was hers, her child, she gave me her wit, her love of wordplay: *If you were all alone on a desert island, and you had brought nothing to eat, how would you survive?* A: You could eat *the sand which is* there! And she taught me to read. She taught all four of her children to read by the age of four or five. She kept each of us with her, forgoing kindergarten. No student was ever better prepared for first grade.

I drew pictures. She encouraged me to write stories to accompany them. "What does the bunny say? Say the bunny says, (in a squeaky voice, her nose wriggling) 'I want a carrot!'"

"I want a carrot!" And she lettered that in a dialogue balloon above the bunny I'd drawn and colored with my brown crayon. From then on, she would only have to point to the words for me to "read" them: *I want a carrot!* Until, one day, I was — was reading them. And she brought me the drawings she had saved and her sewing box, and we stitched them together into books we would show my father when he got home from work.

Together we would make a little man and a little woman of leftover pie dough and toothpicks and bake them in the oven with cinnamon sugar and butter. While we waited for our people to bake, we ate tomato soup and toast. In the spring we would harvest the dandelions in the backyard. The scissors I used to cut them were plastic and fashioned to look like a giraffe.

The nostalgia I feel writing this, for childhood, for being cared for, doted upon by a loving mother, is not the point. But neither is it entirely beside the point: it is a way into memory, the swinging open of a gate to a beckoning, peaceful place, like one of those idyllic city parks we stroll in, which happens of course to be, also, a cemetery.

I was a junior in college with a summer job at Columbia's oceanography lab in Dobbs Ferry, NY, when an opportunity arose to take part in an underwater sound experiment off the Grand Banks. We would be at sea for six weeks in the North Atlantic. I saw this as the adventure of my young life thus far. By then, I was sure I wanted to be a writer, and for a 21 year old guy insecure about his manhood, that meant trying on the romantic costume, the mythology about writers; shipping out, getting your seaman's papers, was a big part of that. But I needed my birth certificate to complete that process so I called my mother who sent it to me.

It was rejected. It was a copy, and they wanted the original. And they needed it by that Friday. It was already Monday! My mother insisted it was the only onc shc had, and the people at the Seamen's Union insisted on either the original or a certified copy from The Commonwealth of Pennsylvania. By Wednesday I was driving my father's car, my mother riding shotgun, on our way to Harrisburg, to acquire the certificate that proved I was born to her. The trip took a little over two hours. It is painful to recall how awkward we were with each other the whole time.

I was annoyed with my mother the whole trip, starting with her saying that she had half a mind to go with me to the union hall and tell them, *See here, I'm the one that lugged him around in my belly and pushed him out into the world and I don't need no piece of paper to prove it. So anything you want to know about him just ask me. I can vouch for him.* I was broke with no money for cigarettes so we both smoked hers, Chesterfield non-filters, stronger than my Marlboros, her cigarette bobbing up and down while she talked, me holding mine in my left hand, occasionally bringing it near the open window to blow the ash from it. I was certain that our discomfort was her backwardness, her boring life; it was her fault we had nothing to talk about. And why did she have to wear those goddamned plastic slippers with the pink flowers on them?

I had already gone from her, already set sail in the great world. It was only natural that I was going to sea, to brave the North Atlantic; no other arena would accommodate my passion, my artist's soul! I was living in a kind of opera in my head. And there I was, needing her. There we were, going to the capitol to certify my birth, together, with nothing to say to each other, with me denying my need for her and, in my young numbness, wholly unaware of her need for me.

I can brave it now, empathy, as I could not have then; I would have been crushed by the weight of her loneliness, not to mention her grief. An old man now, much of my life accomplished, many questions settled for better and for worse, thinking of my mother's life makes me cry. Big boys don't cry, but grown men do. Her terrible loneliness in that kitchen, seated on a cracked vinyl chair at the formica table where a heavy cut-glass ashtray, blackened with sighs, held the evidence of time's passing, of time passing her by. They were all over the house, these ashtrays, seldom washed, begrimed and often full, but somehow unseen, ignored, in a house that my mother otherwise kept spotless.

"Daresn't" is, among other things, a class marker. It is only one of the idiomatic features of my mother's speech, only one of her verbal quirks I often felt ashamed of as I left home and ventured forth. The story of "upward mobility" involves a great deal of self-hatred, a disavowal of the place and people who sustained you, along with denial of that repudiation. Betrayal and shame and defiance and anger, all tumbling over one another, locked in a kind of melee. For years. Then one day, exhausted, you give up, and in that spent state you see that it was all a waste of time and effort: that aspect of self-definition so puny and unimportant compared to other and larger ethical, social, generational matters. That understanding leads you back to an appreciation of the people you left, the people you left "behind" as if there had been, ever, someplace else to go. If you're lucky, it's not too late. I was not lucky.

But why was I hiding in sleep? And in my room? And after all these worldly years of struggle and mirth and rage and joy and wonder? I have learned to surrender to it, this despondency; it doesn't last. I have learned to givc in to it if possible, that it is periodic, not chronic; the weather, not the climate. But that is not how it feels when you are in the middle of it, so I need to remind myself: this too shall pass. Maybe it has always been my mother waking me when the storm has passed, and her audible prohibition this time finally made me aware of her, of her continuing presence.

Should I list here the things that were on my mind just before I folded my hand, not up to the bluff I would need to play on? (When I am in that state, it seems like a bluff, a fake-it-till-you-make-it effort to override the heaviness I feel.) Or should I just describe myself as a man who is trying to make sense of a life that straddles two atrocious centuries, unwilling or unable to continue otherwise? Would that be enough? To say that I could not tune out the hatred and the horror, the way that empathy has all but disappeared behind tall walls and sentinelled gates? Anybody who has been paying attention knows all that, anybody who is awake. Ah. Precisely. And so, I look for peace in sleep, and I can easily saw off 12 or 13 hours at a time.

The continual state of war, the mass incarceration of young people, the violence in our streets, the exploitation of children as trainee consumers and the turning of educational systems into indoctrination centers, the discounting of any and all value that can't be monetized, and on and on. I could make this into a manifesto but I seem to recall the pathetic Ted Kaczinski, a.k.a. the Unabomber, already did that. Nobody read his screed, including me. Besides, I don't seek revenge on anyone, and anyway, it would be like swatting at mosquitoes in a swamp. So I put it aside, retreat, withdraw, put out the light, get the pillows just right and make my escape. A brief vacation in oblivion, a one-night stand with despair.

"Daresn't."

She would never tell me the answer to her riddles, or only begrudgingly after I threatened to cry. *What's black and white and re(a)d all over?* She waited for my answer, smoking. The cigarette was white with black print — well, gray — and the tip glowed red when she inhaled! Nah. That wasn't it.

"A firetruck!"

"Nope."

"Yes it is, Mom! Yes it is!"

"Nope. A newspaper. Get it?"

What has four wheels and flies?

"An airplane!"

"Nope."

I ran to my room to get my toy plane, a Christmas present, to convince her: "See? Here are two wheels under the wings, and then up under the nose are the other two close together! So I'm right! I'm right!"

"Nope." She wanted me to figure out the pun for myself. And I suppose she wanted to teach me to be careful of trick questions, to be aware of how words can fool you. "But what the hell, we can both be right I guess." She stubbed out her cigarette, blew a long cloud of smoke.

So this is an act of conjuring, from memory, from need. Will that be the truth? No. But it will be a portrait, equal parts memory and speculation, and something more substantial at least than a voice in a dream. I can be forgiven for wanting more than that, can't I? For believing that strange word might mean that I daresn't think myself motherless, daresn't think myself deserving only of these few questionable impressions made on a terribly inattentive younger self?

After all, I was able to summon her, to somehow make her present for my children through anecdotes, through our visits to their grandfather, her husband, in the house she lived and died in, through her cake recipe and her favorite foods; of those few things and my children's need for her, I made a hologram, a kindly spectre, Grandma Dolly.

And so, of shards, of patterns, of others' impressions, of light and shade, motes and flecks, I will remember her, reassemble her, the mother I need to wake me as she always did, forbidding my defeat each morning of my sorrowful boyhood, first calling up the stairs to me, then adding a threat, then stomping her way up — *last chance, young man!* — before grabbing my leg and pulling me from the bed onto the cracked linoleum floor.

She didn't know why, at 11 years old, I was already in retreat, in love with oblivion, but she was having none of it; two of her sons were going to die — this one, goddammit, was going to live.

That her voice could come to me so clearly in dream, or in that space between dreaming and waking, surely means that she remains with me, inside me, as her parents reside in her, and so on and so on, particulars faded but certain restive and insistent resolutions persisting: what of her hurts, I wonder, her injuries, remain unhealed, unquieted in me? I suspect now that more important than understanding those bequests is the refusal to be defeated by their attendant sorrows. The first requirement is to get out of bed.

What is broken and beaten but never complains?

ARBOR VITAE

"Trees are Earth's endless effort to speak to the listening heaven."

— Rabindranath Tagore

MY NEIGHBOR ACROSS the street wants to cut down the tree in the front of her house; she says its roots are compromising her foundation, and besides, she wants more sun so she can grow flowers in her front yard. I try to talk with her about it, but find I am surprisingly emotional. A few years earlier my neighbor next door took down a row of white pines between our houses because they were dripping sap on his car in the driveway. I loved them for the way they held the snow in the winter; the windows on that side of the house were like Hiroshige snowscapes. I tried to argue with him when the arborist's truck pulled up and I saw what they were about to do, but I lost. The trees were on his side of the property line, if only by a foot, and he had made up his mind. I steamed about it for a couple of days, but we're a tight little urban neighborhood and holding a grudge was never an option. But here I am nearly begging my neighbor across the street to spare the red maple in front of her house, and I'm surprised at the strength of the feelings that have been stirred in me. I get on my bike and head for the park nearby where I can sit by the lake under a favorite willow and think about it.

The truth is I was feeling a little embarrassed by the whole thing. It was undeniably sentimental; what was the point of arguing about a single tree? I had enjoyed the pines next to my house; I understood my reasons for wishing they'd been left standing. But the truth is that I never really paid the tree across the street much attention. Still, it seemed worthwhile to try to figure out why I felt so desperate on this one little maple's behalf.

Our relationship to trees is a conspiracy, literally. We breathe together. It is symbiosis on a grand scale. Every schoolkid knows this. We take in oxygen and breathe out carbon dioxide. In comes the good air, out goes the bad. Trees are our very life support, and we, along with the other animals, are theirs. We sustain one another, we conspire for the common good of carbon-based life. It only remains to be said that the "spire" in conspire is, etymologically, spirit, the breath without which we would die, and not only metaphorically.

So I see the relationship of people to trees as a conversation that involves quiet, attention, listening. What people have always done with breath, with spirit, is make stories, and I have no reason to believe that trees don't similarly shape their breathing. Trees listen, then they tell their side of the same survival narrative. We have this conversation continuously on the molecular level. When the trees speak they tell me of course of water (they even sometimes make the sound of it quite convincingly.) They also talk about light. When I breathe in deeply in a forest, a light brightens just behind my eyes as surely as I see a canoe when you say the word canoe or conjure my daughter when you speak her name. Trees tell me other things as well; they seem to know me. Sometimes they tell me things that I don't know I've heard until a long time after. Our breathing, I imagine, tells the trees of joy and desire, anger and injury, and is often shaped into the long sighs of sorrow. We tell it all, in every chemical flavor, storytelling virtuosos who by now, after a couple of million years, know how by heart.

It may be that trees have given us language itself. According to Robert Graves, our alphabet, descended from ancient runes, derives from the patterns of branches against the light of the moon; Anglo-Saxon runes were called by the names of trees: elm, beech, birch, locust. I am unwilling to dismiss the idea — it occurs to me too often — that trees are a superior species. According to Andreas Feininger, there are trees on the planet right now more than four thousand years old! Trees may have been the presences who called us from the waters long ago, breathing life into our brachiating lungs, then as now our beckoning siblings, body to body, need to need, gift to gift.

This is why, when I am dispirited, I like to sit in the woods.

And yet, I know that others find this essential conversation elsewhere. My wife prefers to walk the beach in colloquy with water, waves, and tides. She is someone who finds her renewal in motion. "I'm exhausted," she says, "I need to go for a walk." She can walk the sand by the waterline for miles and return somehow unburdened, happy. I suspect this has to do with the years she spent in Sicily as a little girl, and on ships in the Mediterranean, and crisscrossing the Atlantic (her father is a retired ship's engineer); the first whiff of salt and she gets that half-smile on her face and the look of a woman listening carefully for something she can almost but not quite hear.

And under the willow, there by the lake, in the moment just before the feelings are right there with me, fully now, a surge of mourning, a hot splash in my chest, I get it: my spirited defense of my neighbor's tree is not about my metaphysics, but my grief.

The house where I lived, with my parents and three younger brothers, until I was thirteen, was a narrow brick rowhouse that still had one of the old slate sidewalks. The slate was heaved and cracked by the roots of a huge tree that shaded the front of the house. My brother Bobby and I, along with our gang of kids from up and down the street, had always enjoyed it as a challenge, first on our tricycles — you had to get up a good head of steam and you had to lean hard as you crested and bumped over the crack or you'd spill over sideways — and later on our roller skates. My father called it "that damned hemlock" because the roots were working their way into our cellar, threatening the foundation.

So I grew up thinking that the tree was a hemlock, but it could not have been because a hemlock is an evergreen, and this great tree, home-base for all our street games, was deciduous. I realized this only in adulthood, and many years after the tree was cut down. It made me wonder what kind of tree it was that I had leaned against so many times, forehead against the rough bark, hands over my eyes, looking into the dark and counting backward.

The bark was deeply furrowed, coarse enough to tear your knuckles on, and black, but if you broke off a piece it was a burnt orange color and light in your hand like cork. I went to the arboretum. I went to the library. From what evidence I could gather, I decided it was a black walnut. I remembered the hard shriveled nuts and the twigs with their pith like white styrofoam that I carved with my thumbnail. I remember using a hammer to smash open the nuts and more often than not finding the cases mysteriously empty inside. I remember the thrill of discovering, later and all by myself, that a little hole in the shell meant a worm had bored its way inside to eat the nutmeat. Then it was fun to bet with Bobby, for a baseball card, or five penny candies from the corner store, and shatter the nut with a hammer, find it empty, and collect.

But it turned out I was wrong. The black walnut I had remembered was somewhere else on the block. The tree in front of our house, whose roots wormed their way into our cellar, was a linden.

I discovered my mistake years later, using a handbook to identify a tree that grew by the house where I lived then. It was the shape of the leaf that changed my mind. Two memories convinced me. The first was of the branch outside the bedroom Bobby and I shared: the leaves were not the walnut's pinnate frond, but crooked hearts, simple and saw-toothed, that had fixed themselves in my consciousness, bobbing and tossing in the wind through years of now forgotten daydreams. The second memory was of the rusty imprint of a leaf on the smooth slate sidewalk when the ice that had trapped it there melted, a kind of snapshot fossil.

One day I came home to find it had been cut down. I believe I was nine because Bobby, a year younger than me, had just been diagnosed with Muscular Dystrophy, the reason he had become so weak, the reason he fell down all the time and why we couldn't play together outside anymore, why he had been moved from our bedroom downstairs to the first floor, and why he would die before we could be adults together. The stump was nearly two feet across, with a six-inch hole in the middle filled with water and ringed by darker marrow-wood. My feelings surprised me. My father had mentioned it would be cut down. He wanted to be rid of it. "It busts up the sidewalk and that's all we need is for some old lady to fall on her ass and sue us." No doubt I had shrugged.

But seeing the stump, surrounded by sawdust and woodchips, was a different matter. It was shocking and sad at a time when I believed, for reasons it has taken me decades to understand, that it was a betrayal of my family to feel sorrow. I almost cried. I almost mourned. I would have if I had let myself look up to see the blank sky and the looming eaves and the black wires lined with bewildered sparrows.

When the tree was gone, the slate was taken up, the offending roots were cut and removed, and a concrete sidewalk poured. The stump remained, darkening and softening, rainwater held in its hollow center, black as the pupil of an eye. In that dark mirror you could stare directly at the sun, moving among gray clouds, a dull coin pale as the moon.

NEIGHBORS

The apparition of these faces in the crowd —
Petals on a wet, black bough.

— Ezra Pound
"In A Station of the Metro"

BOSTON'S MBTA RED LINE used to end at Porter Square, until recently the town-gown divide in Cambridge, with working people living north of Porter and east into Somerville's Davis Square and Powderhouse neighborhoods. Now it continues to Davis Square, and then on to Alewife Station with its tiered parking garage for commuters from the suburbs. All this change, along with the repeal of rent-control, has transformed the neighborhoods so that Cambridge now has the greatest number of homes worth over a million dollars of any city in the US, and Somerville's Davis Square is going through the familiar transition from workers to artists to money.

Outside Porter Station, a 46-foot tall red steel sculpture, "Gift of the Wind" by Susumu Shingu, makes its benefactor visible in a mesmerizing and graceful kinesis above the plaza. A remarkable work, it seems to allude to a weathervane and ferris wheel and sail and horseshoe crab and lobster all at once while it swivels and dips and turns like a prayer-wheel or thurible, its blessings quintessentially New England.

I love the Red Line's public art. Over at the Davis stop are life-size statues by James Tyler of people he recruited from the neighborhood, and people from out of town are always having their pictures taken with them. The sculptor's given them masks. Tourists pose with them so that their postures blend, to see if they can fool the folks back home, if only for a moment: *Who are those people with you? Why are they wearing masks? Oh.* Elsewhere the art is themed to the stop; at Kendall/M.I.T. for example, the walls chronicle the history of scientific and technological discovery, and a button on the wall activates a series of colliding chimes between the inbound and outbound tracks.

On this particular rainy day, just inside the door of Porter station, the flower vendor has her ephemeral inventory arranged in buckets on risers, but it seems futile: who buys flowers on their way *to* work? At the top of the escalator a man hands each commuter a Metro, a mere outline of a newspaper, little more than headlines and advertising. I take mine and step onto the moving stairs down.

The escalators plunge deep into the earth, the first long ride down bringing you from street level to a plaza with a snack bar, an ATM machine, and a vendor whose cart, depending upon the season, is loaded with baseball caps, sweaters, scarves, gloves, battery operated fans, and of course incense and pre-paid telephone cards. Both vendors, the man with the cart and the man at the snack bar, are clearly Arab, and I have wanted to ask each where he is from but worry the question would seem an affront, my sociable curiosity freighted as it is with history and politics and fear. Everyone is fully aware of the changed context for all our interactions since the bombing in the London tube, but even to talk about that fear openly would brand you a suspicious character. Next to the vendor's cart, a man is selling *Spare Change*, "The Newspaper By For And About The Homeless". He is always there lately, standing with his stack of papers under one arm, holding out a copy to us as we debark the stairs. His left eye may be glass; it stares up and to the left so that the one eye that is fixed on you seems ferocious and accusative. And why should he not be angry? Or his fierce gaze may be serving him as a disguise, a mask suggesting danger, covering his otherwise naked vulnerability. No doubt he is homeless himself, and he seems surrounded by unasked questions about how he came to be here glaring at us and importuning us to buy for a dollar what we wish not to know.

Just ahead of me on the escalator down, a woman is rummaging in a huge purse hanging from her shoulder while her child, a girl about four or five, holds onto the moving black handrail with both hands. This is the next chapter of the descent, an additional hundred and fifty feet or so to the inbound train platform; there's still another level down after that, to the outbound trains. And here's more art: the bronzed gloves of the workers who dug and tunneled and blasted and laid track and tiled and otherwise carved this now taken-for-granted place out of earth and rock not so long ago; there are pairs of them at intervals along the aluminum console that separates the UP and DOWN escalators. The artist, Mags Harries, calls them "narrative sculpture," presumably because they allude to the story of the building of this station, but also because one is led from one glove or pair of gloves to the next as one moves through the narrative of one's own journey. The little girl in front of me notices the first pair and cranes her neck to keep looking as the stairs take her away, and then another pair comes into her view; now she realizes there must be others, too, and she looks both up and down to see where they are. She pulls at her mother's sleeve to show her and her mother says, yes, yes, I see, I see, but she is deep in her bag and isn't looking. Watching this child, I think I understand something; I see that art, this art anyway, can serve to direct our gaze, to somehow help us manage our attention. Art gives us something to do with our voracious eyes; it occupies our thoughts, tempers our anxieties, soothes our discomforts. At least until we get to the platform itself, where commercial space begins, with ads for booze, for dating services, for Christian Fellowship and deodorant.

In some situations, the subway being one of them, it is important to "keep custody of the eyes" as the nuns used to teach my classmates and me in talking about temptations of the flesh. When we were in third or fourth grade we were curious to understand this phrase but still too young to grasp its meaning; later we weren't at all interested. I always figured it meant, sort of, "mind your own business." Once, not long ago, I heard a woman on the street yell at a man, "You keep your goddamned eyes to yourself!" and I couldn't decide whether she was crazy or if the man, who of course gave me an exaggerated innocent shocked look, had been leering at her.

Today the music is provided by a young woman playing the violin, a Bach Partita interrupted by a recorded announcement reminding us that for our safety we should report any unattended packages or suspicious persons to the station manager. Her music is on a stand before her, case open on the floor with a few coins and a couple of bills in it. A few other people have distributed themselves here and there on the platform, some students, an older Asian couple who are both wearing white surgical masks, two mothers with babies in strollers. One of the people looks remarkably like my brother Joe who lives in Pennsylvania and whom I see too seldom. I've been seeing this guy around the neighborhood for years; once when my daughter Veronica was small she grabbed my arm and pulled me down to her to ask, in a hot little whisper, cupping both hands around my ear, "Is that Uncle Joe?" and I had to look hard to assure myself he wasn't my brother. The guy's a dead ringer. Over the years Veronica would tell me now and then that she had seen "the Uncle Joe guy" again.

A few feet away from me on the platform, the woman with the heavy purse — sliding down her arm — grabs the little girl by the wrist and yanks her arm and slaps at her bottom all at once but the little girl, practiced, I guess, in these matters, goes limp and twists herself away from the blow. The mother yanks her back to her feet, "Stand up!" she says. Then she spits on a handkerchief and wipes the child's face with it. "I'm not going to tell you again. You hear me?" The little girl seems far from crying. She doesn't look like she's ever cried in her whole short life. I can see she is watching her mother's hands. Suddenly the mother is looking at me, a glaring challenge: What*chew* lookin' at? As I turn my gaze away I register for the briefest moment that the child is giving me the same look: I've witnessed her shame and now she hates me from behind her mother's leg.

You can feel the train approaching before you hear it or see its light in the tunnel because it pushes air ahead of it into the station. I take out my iPod, put in my earbuds, choose some Thelonious Monk for the ride, and as the train pulls into the station, I check my watch, which is always set ten minutes fast, a strategy that depends on my fooling myself all day long.

I generally look for that single seat in the corner of the car, and it was free, not many people on the train yet since Porter is only the third stop. Monk was laying down a deep melodic and harmonic framework, a starting point for his explorations, and I took out my paperback of *The Idiot*, settled my half-lenses on my nose, and looked forward to picking up the story of Prince Myshkin where I'd left off the day before. Of course as we entered the tunnel I checked myself out in the dark mirror of the window across from me, a ritual of self consciousness I try to keep in check. And then I looked around at the others, wearing the most unthreatening look I could muster. To my left was a young man, well-dressed, with a leather briefcase flat on his lap. Across from me was a man sprawled across three or four seats, sleeping I supposed. Among the other thirty or forty people in the car there seemed to be four or five different uniforms, depending on race, class, and occupation. Though some people dress to call attention to themselves, to stand out, most people dress to blend in, to become invisible. In the middle of the car was a man impeccably outfitted and assiduously groomed but whose hair was clearly not his own; in fact, it didn't much look like hair at all. The way he was glaring at himself in the window, brushing at his coif with his hand, made him seem mercilessly impatient with himself, a miserable sort of narcissism I thought, as if his attempts to make himself blend in and become acceptably invisible had backfired and he wondered why it wasn't working, why everyone was still, well, giving him those *looks*. He caught me gazing at him, looked away, reached under the seat for a discarded newspaper to read.

Can a person *feel* a look? Of course he can. In situations like this, when we are together not by choice but by necessity, we get nervous, we get on one another's nerves, and our sense of personal boundaries becomes acute. Decorum requires nearly absolute self-containment, and the lack of privacy feels threatening. Both observer and observed are caught in a double bind. We're not supposed to stare; in fact, our stolen looks, like shots made with a secret camera, prove our implacable desire, our utter fascination with one another. Fortunately, there's art. What else could possibly aid us in averting our gaze, brimming with curiosity, judgment, desire, and fear, but art? What else is more interesting than other human beings except, perhaps, the things human beings make to look at, touch, read, hear? Thelonious Monk was just unravelling the melody like taking apart an elegant theorem while pleasurably demonstrating how the parts might be reconfigured to create a different mood, even a different set of premises from which to start over. Without entirely intending to, I looked at myself in the window again. I assessed what I saw there: not an unpleasant face, better from the left because my nose is crooked, beard needs a trim, hairline receded but in a way that seemed all right to me, forehead high and shiny, smart, mature. I was wearing my nobody's fool expression, and trying, I think, to avoid the image just behind the image of myself, the blackness roaring there. Maybe that roaring is behind every image we have of ourselves. One thing is for certain, anyone who thinks his reflection in a piece of glass is what other people see when they look at him is even a bigger fool than he is a narcissist.

I tried to return to the story of Myshkin; I was just picking up at the part when Roghozin attempts to murder him, but we were slowing down and soon had pulled into Harvard

Station. As people came through the door, they looked at the seats across from me where the man was sprawled, and moved away to find seats elsewhere. I think this was what first got my attention, and I noticed that the man sprawled across from me seemed not to be merely sleeping. For one thing, his posture wasn't that of someone trying to make himself comfortable — one arm was hooked behind the seats at an angle that made me wince to see it, and his other arm was folded behind him. His head was lolled back, mouth open, the whites of his eyes visible under half-shut lids. His skin had the color and granular look of the inside of a baked potato, and his lips were chalky white. All in all there was an alarming rigidity about him. About a dozen people came into the car, people with shopping bags, with newspapers folded just-so to the articles they were reading, students with backpacks, a mother with a child in a stroller. I watched each register discomfort with the ghastly body angled across the seats as they moved away.

As the doors closed, I looked to my left at the young man with the leather briefcase in his lap who had been watching me take in the scene, and now he gave me a conspiratorial smirk, a look that said, "It takes all kinds...," a look that asked for reassurance that whatever kind we were we were different from whatever kind he was over there across from us looking like a broken puppet. I looked from the young man to others around us. A smirk from a young woman, clearly a student, who went back to highlighting her spiral-bound text. A dark-skinned woman, her hair in cornrows and with enormous rings on several of her fingers avoided eye contact with me and was moving her lips, perhaps praying, maybe in another language. I thought the unconscious man was breathing, that I could see his chest rise and fall. But then I wasn't sure if it wasn't simply the rocking of the train. A man in business attire except for a Red Sox cap caught my eye; he raised his eyebrows, gave me a tight-lipped smile, looked over at the sprawled man, back at me, and shook his head.

I have never been especially squeamish. Even in school, back in the first grade, I was the one — along with my friend Patrick McFadden — who the nun would send to the janitor's closet for the bag of sawdust and the spaghetti mop and the wheeled pail with wooden rollers whenever one of my classmates threw up. And in college, for a time I worked as an ambulance attendant in the Bronx, back in the days when the only certification you needed was a card from the Red Cross and a strong stomach. No, the force-field around this man was an entirely different kind of fear.

Somehow, with more of us in the car, the looks that went around began to take on a multiplicity of meanings, shot through with distaste, disapproval, annoyance, and a little panic, as if to say, "Isn't there somebody here who can take care of this?" Monk by now had the melody in pieces spread out like an exploded diagram so that if you hadn't listened from the beginning it would be nothing but chaos, noise. We all wanted someone official, someone who worked for the transit authority, maybe a cop, to clear up the question of whether the broken man was alive or dead and to remove the offending item of his contorted body and slack-jawed awful face. The train continued on its way. I looked and looked. I turned off Monk who was by then raging against the rules of harmony, asking if they were for real, and put the earbuds and my book in my bag. I was already in motion, I can see now, even though I didn't really know what I was going to do, or even that I was going to do anything at all. The situation was simply intolerable. An ad above the inanimate man read DO YOU SUFFER FROM DEPRESSION? with an 800 number to call, and on a larger placard beside him, next to the window, a school promised to change one's career prospects but there were none of the paper tear-off applications left. The man did not appear drunk to me. I thought that he might be an addict overdosed on heroin. Or an Oxycontin casualty. He was dressed in clothing sensible for winter, with none of the signs of one who lives on the streets.

I got up and lurched the few steps across the car; holding onto the horizontal pole above him I leaned over. "Sir? Sir! Are you okay?" I chided myself, *Oh yeah, he's great. Never felt better.* I looked at his sallow skin and his slack jaw; his eyes rolled back in his head, little crescents of white visible where the lids were not quite shut. The last guy I saw who looked this bad was dead, I thought, and it was true. A woman in the Bronx had called for an ambulance after coming home from work to find her husband dead in his barcalounger, evidently for several hours. He had stiffened in the shape of a shallow Z. We couldn't use the stretcher and had to take him down by making a seat of our clasped arms.

This close I was able to see that the man was breathing. I looked up and everyone was watching us. Now there was drama. The young man with the briefcase made a face at me that I took to mean, "Don't bother. He's a doper. Let him sleep it off." Others gave me that sneer and shake of the head that seems to accompany the attitude of superiority. A tall man came toward me, clearly a workman, with plaster-spattered, rust-colored clothing and molded knee-pads now slipped down to his calves, his leather tool-bag slung over one shoulder. "Is he breathing?"

"Barely. But I can't get any response from him. Sir!" I barked at him again.

"Let's try and sit him up. Hey buddy. Hey, come on now, let's try to sit you up." I managed to free the arm from behind the seat. The hand was cold and the arm was stiff. The workman was holding the man's head straight and tapped him, gently, on his clean-shaven cheek. His eyelids twitched just slightly. "Hey buddy, you with us? Can you hear me?" The man seemed to be trying unsuccessfully to regain consciousness.

At the next station, Central Square, I stepped out onto the platform; there's always a brakeman somewhere midway in the train who sticks his head out and looks up and down the platform before closing the doors, and when I was sure he saw me, I waved my arms and pointed into the car with both hands. I waved and waved at him, but I wasn't sure he was going to do anything; he pulled his head back into the car. The workman, still holding the other man upright, looked to me for information and I shrugged. I felt prissy in my sport jacket and topcoat, stupid and ineffectual. Then I noticed the callbox a few steps away, next to the door between cars: three louvred slots above a red button. I pressed it and heard a crackling sound. I wasn't sure it was working, and I also found myself wordless: I didn't want to say that someone was sick in our car; that would sound like somebody'd puked and I didn't think that would be taken very seriously. I said, "Excuse me. Someone is very ill here. We have a medical emergency in our car." There was no answer.

I sat next to the unconscious man to help prop him up. Although the man had not regained consciousness, the workman kept talking to him in a warm and soothing voice. "You just hang in there, buddy. It's gonna be all right. Just hang in there, okay?" The callbox crackled and a voice said, "Hello? Hello? Can I help you?" just as a uniformed man I recognized as the brakeman I'd been waving at entered the car. "What's the trouble here?"

I happened to see, behind him, a look of exasperated disgust on the face of a man who, exhaling loudly through his nose, made a big fuss of looking at his watch.

"I'm not sure," I said. "This man's not well."

The brakeman's face had a strangely skeptical look on it, as if we might all be playing a joke on him. Finally he spoke into his walky-talky: "Yes. This is seven nine. We have a situation here. Central Station. Caucasian male, unconscious, appears to be sick or intoxicated. Requesting medical assistance."

The unconscious man seemed to stiffen and his head rolled back. The workman opened the man's jacket and loosened his collar. "No no. Stay with us, buddy. Stay with us," the workman said, and he held the man's head upright, his face between his hands as if he meant to kiss him, his thumb moving on the man's cheek below his eye, for reassurance.

The callbox beside the door was crackling, "Hello? Did you call for assistance? Hello?" The brakeman ignored it, so I pressed the red button and said that help had arrived. In fact, it was another ten minutes or so before three EMTs lugging boxes, oxygen, a folding stretcher, arrived. The leader of the group proceeded to take his futile turn at rousing the man, and he almost managed, too; there seemed something in his voice that was calling the man forth from wherever he was up there where his eyeballs had rolled. To me, the man's voice made questions sound like commands, an assertive concern asking, in a deep baritone, for help in solving a problem he and the patient had in common, and I could see the man trying to open his eyes. Then, softly but clearly, he said, "Gerald," though his eyes remained closed.

"Is that your name, sir? Gerald? Gerald? Can you hear me? Do you take any medications, Gerald? Any medicine? Gerald?"

The man shook his head from side to side and said, "No," in what was somehow only half a syllable. One of the EMTs already had Gerald's coat off and sleeve rolled up, caressing his forearm as if to rub the circulation back into it. I thought he was looking for heroin tracks. "Gerald, we're going to start an IV. Gerald. Try and stay with us, Gerald." He called the brakeman over and they conferred. Then the brakeman turned to us, "Let's give these men the room they need to work, okay? Move back everyone. Give them room." A number of people, already impatient, hoping no doubt the EMTs would carry the man off the train so we could be on our way, groaned at the implication we would be stuck there for awhile, and the man I'd noticed looking at his watch harumphed off the train, flashing me a glare and muttering he would try to find a cab. Most of us moved away, to the other end of the car, including the tall workman with the kneepads. I only moved a step or two away myself. I felt a little proprietary; after all, I was the one who had set this all in motion. I thought that maybe the EMTs would have some questions for me. When the brakeman took a step toward me and said, "Sir, we need you to move away and give these men room to work," I felt insulted. How dare he talk to me as if I were an obstacle? Wasn't I the one who'd summoned him? Didn't I earn the right to learn the outcome of this situation?

As I moved away, one of the EMTs was looking in Gerald's wallet. He pulled out a card, "There it is," he said, "diabetic."

"I'm already on it," said the man on one knee by the first -aid box. "Gerald, we've started an IV. Gerald can you hear me? Hang on, pal. We're going to get you through this."

As I walked deeper into the car people looked at me and then away into newspapers, books, puzzles. Maybe three or four minutes later, the brakeman instructed us to evacuate and move to one of the adjoining cars. I met eyes for a moment with the tall workman, and though I cannot explain it, his look managed to communicate to me what these new instructions must have meant: either there had been a sudden crisis, a heart attack or stroke, or Gerald was dead. Once again, we were momentarily co-conspirators, savvy, in-the-know, and I wanted to cut through the crowd and talk to him, but the look he'd given me had also somehow put that off limits.

At Kendall the platform was quite full; the train was late and as it slowed to a stop I could see the impatience and anxiety in peoples' faces and postures. The car filled.

Soon we were rising into the light and over the Longfellow Bridge, its four stone towers giving it character beyond its function. An Anglo-American bridge, unlike the bridges of Paris, say, or Prague, it makes no promises of angelic protection. It was a gray day but the rain turned the river to a beautiful infinity of intersecting rings. When the recorded voice intoned "Charles MGH. Mass. General Hospital" and we pulled alongside the crowded, elevated platform, I wondered if the EMTs would have taken Gerald off the train back at

Central, or continued until now, which seemed to me to be a faster, surer route to the hospital than an ambulance through city streets.

When you leave Charles MGH you accelerate past a brick apartment building very close to the tracks, and just when you are about to get a glimpse of somebody's kitchen, you're plunged into darkness and your own reflection again and the train descends on its way to Park Street. By the time our tightly packed train pulled into the crowded station, passengers were readying to debark in a hurry. The doors first open on one side then the other, and I moved with the crowd onto the center platform, making our way through the reluctantly parting throng of passengers waiting to board. A man behind me bumped me, hard, as he went past, in a way that may well have been deliberate. I moved away from the train and turned to look back at the car still emptying like a burst pod, the new passengers beginning to surge forward, and I noticed that the next car back, the one on which I'd started my commute, was still closed to riders, and I wondered what that meant. Above the track, a great bronze hand, one of a pair comprising Ralph Helmick's sculpture "Benedictions", in the unmistakable sign of blessing, bestowed its peace on every single one of us. I looked at my watch, but I knew the time was wrong.

A KIND OF SORCERY: On Shame, Defiance, And Moral Imagination

for Linda McCarriston

A HALF-CENTURY AGO, Kurt Vonnegut, in *Slaughter-house Five*, wrote:

> America is the wealthiest nation on Earth, but its people are mainly poor, and poor Americans are urged to hate themselves.... It is in fact a crime for an American to be poor, even though America is a nation of poor. Every other nation has folk traditions of men who were poor but extremely wise and virtuous, and therefore more estimable than anyone with power and gold. No such tales are told by American poor. They mock themselves and glorify their betters.

In the US, the dominant class narrative is the story of the individual rising from humble origins to take his or her place in the halls of power, whether in government, industry, or the academy. Many of us who were leveraged into buying this bill of goods believed we could make our own separate peace with it, that we could learn to cross easily back and forth across the border between our origins in poor and working class families and the middle-class world to which we aspired and became acculturated. It has taken a long time and a good deal of psychic dissonance to learn that there are checkpoints on both sides of that border and that by crossing it we have incurred suspicion if not outright wrath that ensures that we will never be at home in either of the worlds in which we move.

In *Half the House*, my memoir of growing up in the industrial city of Allentown, Pennsylvania in the fifties and sixties, I wrote this about my mother:

> My mother's voice, her "dutch" accent, is hard to render on the page. The pitch and lilt of the Pennsylvania Dutch accent is, I think now, beautiful for its tone of innocent questioning, the voice generally swelling once about mid-sentence before concluding like a question even when it isn't. Not to mention the integrity of its stubbornly German syntax. I didn't always think so, however, and thinking of the years I spent as a young man trying to shed that inflected speech, I am struck by how pervasive was my mother's influence on me, not to mention the persistence of her shame. She was stuck between not wanting to talk "dutchified" and not wanting to sound "citified" which she was afraid would be construed as putting on airs.
>
> My mother taught me to devalue her. Even that sentence — let it stand — blames her for everything, including the shame I feel for having been ashamed of her. I grew up watching which fork the others were using, what they were wearing, what they were talking about, what they seemed to be thinking. They, whoever they happened to be, had the power to find us wanting. "I'm not going to take you anywhere anymore unless you learn how to behave."

So I set out to "learn how to behave," to acquire what Marx called "cultural capital," which I now understand means mostly affability and white skin. I was developing the former; the latter I already had. I have come to believe that this aspiration, encapsulated in the phrase "upward mobility" is rooted in shame and, in its undermining of authentic selfhood, creates a raw vulnerability ripe for exploitation by all manner of predators from child molesters to military recruiters to advertisers to political candidates and financial institutions.

Not long ago I was talking with the memoirist and essayist Joe Mackall. We were laughing and commiserating about how we had come to be viewed by our blue-collar families and the people with whom we'd grown up. I told Joe about showing up to visit my aunt soon after I'd published my memoir. She opened her door and said, "Oh bless you, you still come to visit your family even after all that money!" Trust me, there was no money. We thought we ought to gather together other writers who found themselves in the same strange, often painful DMZ in the class war and offer it as a panel. At one point I asked Joe how we would figure out who to ask to join us. He said, "Well, if you're all fucked up about who you are and where the hell you fit in but everybody back home thinks you're a big success, you qualify." Sage words.

Some years ago, I agreed to take part in just such a panel discussion about working class academics at a local liberal arts college. Three of us sat facing perhaps twenty or thirty professors who'd brought their lunch trays to the conference room where the discussion was to be held. We kicked it off with a 10 minute introductory statement from each of us. I said I wanted to talk about shame as an integral structural element of the class system, and I read a few pages of something I was working on.

What we thought might easily become too abstract and academic soon became an unburdening for many as professor after professor talked about having working class origins, of being the first in their families to go to college, of feeling they were masquerading among colleagues who, they assumed, were descended from a long line of middle-class professionals. The most unlikely people dropped the charade — granted it was a self-selecting group since attendance was voluntary — and it turned out that the room was filled with people who had been hiding from one another, ashamed, not only camouflaged by their own devices, but also by projecting nearly patrician identities onto all the others, and at a college whose pay scale rates among the lowest 10% of four-year schools (yet another cause for shame.) There were tears. Clearly people were shaken by even the beginnings of a discussion of class. At one point, one professor, a music historian whose specialty is opera, asked if we didn't think that these estrangements and feelings of fraudulence and insecurity were not, after all, just part of human nature.

That's when my own tears surprised me; nothing dramatic, but my eyes welled as I blurted, "It is not human nature to be ashamed of your own mother." Nor, I might have added, to come to your senses only after she was dead and then be ashamed you were ever such a patronizing little twit to have been ashamed of her, and to be ashamed that somehow you'd allowed yourself to be jived into this scam, convinced you were "moving up," and that it wasn't a betrayal, only a bettering of your circumstances, exactly what she always wished for you.

The music professor looked stricken, and I worried that I'd been rude to her. But when she spoke again, she talked about being the daughter of a long-haul truckdriver. And she wept.

What is the cost of this "passing"? What is the cost of this masquerade to "first generation" college students? Having been one of them, albeit a long time ago, I believe I can now see how I was being erased, how identifying with my own origins left me with only shame or defiance as choices. How choosing shame, not defiance, was prescribed. How shame was what the new life cost. How I paid it.

And I recognized this dynamic as abusive, as the continuing consequence of abuse.

Bear with me, please, while I try to describe and understand the unchanging relationship between the powerful and powerless, and the shame that is both its product and its sustenance. Wherever I look at institutional dynamics, religious organizations, prescribed roles, I see the same pattern repeating like a Mandelbrot fractal.

When I was a kid, like a significant cohort of my generation who have at last begun to speak about it, I was exploited for sex by a man who performed the priestly function of "coach." Sports were the way up and out, and up and out was where we were aimed by our teachers and parents, by television's promises, by definitions of power, sex, respectability. The alternative was to join the ranks of the uncles working at Mack trucks, or Bethlehem Steel, or Air Products. Why this was such a terrible fate was never clear to me as a child, but it was clearly the fall-back position, what you settled for if you failed to achieve escape velocity, and for boys from poor families like mine, that escape meant getting an athletic scholarship to college.

College itself was a mythical land of tweeds and muted plaids and leather-bound books, a world of rolling green lawns and trees, and buildings that reeked of knowledge and wisdom, with arcane symbols on coats of arms bearing Latin inscriptions, and thick, green ivy climbing the walls. It was mythical because no one I knew had ever been there. There were a few older guys who went away on football scholarships, but they weren't part of my circle, and besides, they never returned home except for brief visits with their families. Once in a while we'd catch sight of them and they looked as changed as we expected them to be, in ways that we could not have put words to.

My father told me he'd been scouted, a left-handed pitcher, by the St. Louis Cardinals and had been invited to training camp. He lasted three days before they sent him home, crushed. "I was back home quicker than a cup of coffee!" he always joked. I grew up hearing this story and it always ended with a sigh: "They gave me a shot. I can't complain. I had my shot." And I would nod, but what I took away was the sigh.

So when I say that this coach performed a priestly function, I mean that he was a powerful figure in a realm sacred to us as boys, a man with the power to help us plan our escape into the broader world, the one who would help us gain a berth on the high school team, first step to the stardom that would attract the recruiters, the guys with the tuition waivers, the first of many, many gate-keepers who might call us "up" to the Varsity, to the Scholarship, to the Majors, the Pros. "Hey kid, look sharp out there. I heard there was a guy maybe comin' to look at you tonight." It was from the larger system of hierarchical gatekeepers that he derived his power over us.

I have written about this period before and at length, in a memoir, and in other essays, and I won't repeat myself here. Suffice to say that as a boy who desperately wanted to play in the starting line-up, move to the high school a known prospect, and land a college scholarship (the whole of it laid down clear as the tracks my father laid for Bethlehem Steel, swinging a sledge eight hours a day) my "choices" were to suck the coach's cock or let him fuck me in the ass.

Shame whispers: I shouldn't be saying this.
Defiance roars: I have the right to say this!
Moral Imagination insists: No one should have this to say.

In the thirty years since I first wrote about this experience, I have served on task forces, citizens' advocacy groups, and government commissions on sexual violence and exploitation of children. I have become acquainted with survivors in Europe, Asia, Africa, South America, Australia, New Zealand and Afghanistan, and have heard their stories of disempowerment, helplessness, and shame. I have witnessed heroes turning their outrage into defiance and political action on behalf of children — not your children or my children, children.

In the circles in which I moved then, among researchers, social workers, psychologists, and lawmakers, issues of class were seldom raised. It seemed to be taboo, in fact, because the official stance, meant to be inclusive of all children's vulnerability, is that childhood sexual abuse cuts across every category; well, of course it does, it does; at the same time, I can't help but think that, just as with other forms of violence, the weight of numbers falls disproportionately on the most defenseless. All children are vulnerable, but the most vulnerable are those already shamed, already compromised by the shame of being poor. Those children are of course the least likely to tell, so they are the ones most often targeted.

This situation appears to be true globally. For example, the UK Parliament not long ago published a report that chronicles widespread sexual exploitation in the global aid community, including organizations like Oxfam, Save the Children, and even the U.N. itself. The number of children exploited and assaulted among the refugee population (currently the largest mass migration in human history) is staggering. Everywhere in the wake of disaster and war, traffickers arrive with the other vermin to profit from the misfortune of the most vulnerable of those displaced — children.

Shame whispers: I shouldn't be saying this.
Defiance roars: I have the right to say this!
Moral Imagination insists: No one should have this to say.

All the various reactions I might have had to the coach's violations, the ways I might have felt about what was happening, were forbidden to me. I was convinced it was wrong to be angry; if I expected to be forgiven on Saturday after confession (the vague "I committed impure acts" was usually all that was required to say) then I had to find it in my heart to forgive. Besides, "feeling sorry for yourself" was probably the very worst character flaw with which one could be charged, no matter what. You could be bleeding to death, but "feeling sorry for yourself" removed, instantly, any grounds you might have for sympathy, even from yourself. "Dwelling on the past" once it was over — "over" beginning immediately, with the next instant, with a fly being zipped, pants being pulled up — was being a crybaby. No sense crying over spilled cum.

And there was no refusing because there were no grounds for refusal. If I refused, "Why not?" was the response, and I could never formulate an answer. "I don't want to" was insufficient: "What do you mean you don't want to? You don't want to! Who the fuck asked you what you want? Get over here!" The abuse of a child is the elemental instance of might makes right, of the prerogatives of hierarchical privilege.

"I knew," writes George Orwell in "Such, Such Were the Joys," his essay about being a scholarship kid at a fancy boys' school, "that bed-wetting was (a) wicked and (b) outside my control. The second fact I was personally aware of, and the first I did not question. It was possible, therefore, to commit a sin without knowing that you committed it, without wanting to commit it, and without being able to avoid it. Sin was not necessarily something that you did: it might be something that happened to you." What's more, you are invited to be sorry for having once been that self, ashamed, and therefore silenced, and to believe you can turn yourself into someone else. *I shouldn't be saying this.*

But if one is wrong to be angry, and wrong not to forgive, and wrong to grieve what was lost, then one is forbidden to spit out the foul seed of abusive power by the only reflexes nature gives us.

No wonder people so often choose to zone out, to be fucked from behind as it were, to choose not to see what's happening. You can try to relax, you can think of something else, maybe watch TV: sports, comedies, soaps, whatever's your pleasure (another integral property of personhood forever redefined by atrocity: in the aftermath of trauma pleasure becomes a synonym for relief.) You tell yourself: *Not so bad. Not as bad. At least. It could be worse. Not bad.* Even *Thank god.*

These are our resigned responses to choices that are always offered in twos, as if we couldn't handle any broader array of options — It's the two party system. It's us or them. It's take the shitty job or starve. It's my way or the highway. It's coercion and exploitation disguised as consent. It's hatred or forgiveness. It's all the same: it's suck or get fucked.

Of that false choice, repeated, rationalized, disguised, denied, is the world of powerlessness established. When the prerogatives of the powerful masquerade as morality, a kind of sorcery happens, it seems, and people fall into shame as if under a spell, into a world in which it makes sense *to mock oneself and glorify one's "betters."* Convinced that a choice between abuses is as good as it gets, the shamed seek favor, time and again, with murderous demagogues. Ultimately this is the world of dictators, armaments, marching armies.

I shouldn't be saying this. I should come up with another metaphor, one that won't make readers cringe. I could say that a child exploited for sex is a raindrop mirroring the whole defeated world; that would be a little more lyrical. Or I could say that surely we all see that it is the same fire, following the same laws, that burns down a house and a city. I could argue that just because a thing is metaphorical does not mean it stops being real, or I could argue that everything in a remembered childhood is metaphorical.

Or I could dispense with metaphor and say, simply, that the abuse of a child is the elemental instance of abusive power and therefore reveals its dynamics. Or just say that the whole of the present order of things depends on those dynamics, even to the extent that some people are still permitted to own other people because they are able to command their time, and our lives just happen to be made of that — time.

2

> What aristocratic writers take from nature gratis, the less privileged must pay for with their youth. Try and write a story about a young man—the son of a serf, a former grocer, choirboy, schoolboy and university student, raised on respect for rank, kissing the priests' hands, worshipping the ideas of others, and giving thanks for every piece of bread, receiving frequent whippings, making the rounds as a tutor without galoshes, brawling, torturing animals, enjoying dinners at the houses of rich relatives, needlessly hypocritical before God and man merely to acknowledge his own insignificance — write about how this young man squeezes the slave out of himself drop by drop and how, on waking up one fine morning, he finds that the blood coursing through his veins is no longer the blood of a slave, but that of a real human being.
>
> — Anton Chekhov

I was complaining to a friend about how hard writing is, and one of the hardest parts of making that claim is the shame I feel making it: after all, my grandfather was a coal miner, my father a steel-worker, among other jobs. My dad and uncles used to goof on me: "Look at him," my father would say, "he sits on his ass for a living!" My uncles, who worked at Mack trucks on the assembly line, would grin and snort. "He might be working right now for all we know," my father smirked, "What do you say? You working over there?"

It was resentment tempered by admiration of a sort and — understandable in men with back trouble, knee trouble, neck trouble, all the result of hard wear and tear on their bodies — a begrudging envy (*That ain't workin'/That's the way you do it/ You play your guitar/On the MTV.*) The whole thing was complicated and there was nowhere else to take it, nothing else to say, so everyone laughed, including me. Somebody popped another can of beer.

"You're a good sport, kid," my uncle Francis said and smacked me across the back of the head. It meant I wasn't thin-skinned, that no matter how far away I'd gone, I was still a member of the tribe who "mock themselves and glorify their betters." I can still feel that slap.

I went off to college and soon after to teach at a prestigious boarding school. On my visits home, the stories I brought with me to tell my father and my uncles required carefully landing on the right side of a class divide that would determine whether they felt proud of me or ashamed of themselves, whether they became appreciative or angry. It often involved my mugging and goofing on the rich — pointing out either a foible that would suggest they are foolish and blind to their own nonsense, or that they are just like us, proving by anecdote another of my father's maxims: "He puts his pants on one leg at a time same as the rest of us." (This bromide was offered by numerous coaches as well, especially if we were going up against a superior team: "Remember they pull up their jockstraps same as you.")

Just as that work my dad and uncles did was hard on their bodies, mine is hard on my sense of myself, my consciousness of the world and my place in it. I am continually trying to lay bare assumptions, making complicated and nuanced choices about how to name a thing, whether it be an emotion, an event, an interaction, some change I've noticed. I take saying no again and again to received formulations to be the job. It's like being a TSA worker on red alert: I have to take the wand to nearly every idea to be sure it isn't smuggling some other suggestion or some unintended, potentially harmful residue of shame. *Are these the right words? Are they true?*

No doubt all writers, all artists, have this struggle to some degree. But if you are a writer from the working class, if you grew up in a house without books, you are never sure that what you do is work at all, and you are seldom sure that, whatever it might be called, you have any right to do it, nor even any right to have the time to do it. I suspect something like this is true for anyone from a poor or working class background, whether or not they are a writer: there is defiance in making anything — song, poem, birdhouse, quilt, trout flies, model trains — anything that isn't done for money. In fact, for nearly anyone these days to try to clear a little space in which to think clearly or make something you find beautiful, whatever it might be, requires defiance and an audacity that will be viewed as selfish by some and will trigger envy and malice in others. The class system, along with its resentments, bullying, and ridicule, is replicated within each class. Defiance is necessary. Defiance is your friend.

Until it isn't. You can try to balance out shame with achievement, but the defiant rage that stokes that kind of ambition burns hotter with every failure, and shame doubles down each time and raises the stakes.

Shame's cascading implosion of selfhood delivered me to alcohol as if it had been waiting for me: liquid defiance, potable rage, lots of it, and more and more of it as time went on. I used to sit at my desk with a rocks glass of scotch in one hand and my pen in the other, defying the shame I felt by insisting I was my own invention: a writer! Never mind that I wasn't writing. Never mind that this invention was itself a cliché, a cartoon, right down to the cigarettes and booze it needed and justified; never mind that I produced little, then very little, then nothing. If I could only manage to write a book, I would prove I was not as worthless as I felt!

The whole of my encounter with myself was this oscillating shame and defiance. I saw this most clearly when, after years of daily drinking, I managed to get sober. I'd been abstinent only two or three weeks when I agreed to go with my wife to a party. I don't remember the occasion, but it was a gathering of people who all knew the host, though few knew one another. I could taste the anxiety in every introduction. I was offered the choice of beer or wine "and there are soft drinks in the kitchen for the children." I was miserable and trying to be invisible, even disappearing for a while into the bathroom, until another guest knocked. After awhile, I looked around the room at people laughing, talking, each with a cocktail or glass of wine in hand, and tried to get my bearings. I wanted desperately to feel something besides the shame I believed everyone could see smeared all over me like shit. I stood in a corner speaking to no one. The inner dialogue then went something like this:

Shame: Why would any of these people want to talk to a loser like me? Even I don't like me!

Defiance: Nah. Fuck that. Look at these superficial fools, laughing like hyenas, talking about nothing — why would I want to talk to any of them?

(repeat)

I was a screeching seesaw, a devil's ping-pong game, my sick sense of self inflating and deflating. The only relief I could imagine was the cartoonish self I'd been imagining at my writing desk: one day I would walk into a party like this and conversations would stop, heads would turn, whispers would be heard: *Look! It's him! I heard he was going to be here!*

A pathetic insight, this flash of the truth I got standing alone, isolated and oscillating in that corner: I saw how fearful and small and self-involved I'd become, but somehow this understanding didn't trip me back into shame this time, but instead suggested it was possible to live — and maybe even write — some other way, that this pathetic psychodrama, now visible for the first time (I almost laughed out loud with relief) was where shame, compounded by alcohol (which had long since stopped helping me) had me cornered.

I stopped writing. Actually, what I stopped was the shame and defiance cockfight. There followed years of 12-Step meetings, of psychotherapy; years of simply not running away into that old boozy delusion. Once, in conversation, a friend, also a recovering alcoholic writer who'd grown up poor, stunned me with the clarity of her assessment — "Richard," she said, 'Great American Writer' is the face of your disease." She cautioned me about ever assuming that aspirational identity again, calling it a seat at the bar with my name on it.

In hindsight, the trouble was that I hadn't been writing to any purpose except to work myself up to believing I was someone I was not. Once off the seesaw, out of the ping-pong game, I began, slowly, to stay in my life, where things had improved a hundredfold without my noticing, a life for which I had considered myself ineligible. I filled notebooks with memories and questions. I wrote a "4th Step Inventory" in which I listed my failings and resolved to make amends, along with a daily "10th Step" journal, reviewing my own behavior that day.

After a few years, I began writing again: poems, stories, a memoir. I wrote to try to shorten the interval between my experience and my understanding of it, not to be that guy who stopped conversations when I walked into the room. I have not, ever since, wanted to cram myself back into that tiny box of imagined importance, dark and smelly as a confessional.

> *Shame whispers: Now you're just trying to elevate your own imposter syndrome to some broader cultural criticism. You can't write about class and hierarchy and history with your only bona fides being that you grew up poor, were raped, and became a drunk!*

Shut up, shame.

Are these the right words? Are they true? I write to see if I can find among all the thoughts in my head which ones are mine, which ones are me, thinking. My consciousness is like a jukebox or mail server or cloud domain that contains a staggering amount of utter crap, useless spam, old pop tunes, bad ideas that just go on and on, unpurged. What I hear when I listen, pen paused above the page, refusing, refusing, tuning out the noise, might be what is actually mine to say. I write to judge the plausibility of explanations I've been offered. I write to try to bring the past into the present in hopes of a glimpse of the future. I write to find the words, to come to terms. I write to stop being a good sport. The ultimate foolishness would be to try as hard as I do to say what I mean and then not mean what I say.

3

I have been avoiding writing about what I'll call my "poverty teeth." I was nearly seventy by the time I had the money to get my teeth fixed. For people living paycheck to paycheck, poverty teeth can be a powerful source of shame. In movies and television, the simplest and most common signifier of poverty and the ignorance that supposedly accompanies it, the fastest way to prompt ridicule, is missing or rotting teeth, or even just crooked teeth. Usually this goes unremarked as a class signifier, but only because it has become so expected, so ubiquitous.

My parents both had dentures. I still remember the day my father came home from the dentist with his mouth stuffed with bloodied gauze. How old was I? 12 or 13, I think. We had just moved, my parents going deeper into debt than they already were in order to buy my grandfather's house from my father's four siblings. Subject to the approval of the Mayor, with whom he had to interview in three weeks time, my father had a shot at an administrative job with the city,

After a period of pain and acute shame that kept him at home, "sick" for a few days, he had a beautiful smile – of removable porcelain teeth. He got a credit card, bought a suit and a sport coat, quit smoking cigarettes, took up a pipe. He got that job, and he gave it thirty years of his life, work he was proud of, but he always remained ashamed of his teeth, worried they might shift or slip, revealing his secret. You could tell because he felt the need to joke about it.

Shame is inescapable it seems, insidious, shape-shifting. Shame is not merely a feeling or a mental state; it is an entanglement in which each and every attempt to avoid it creates another occasion for it. Its consequence, defiance, is the other side of the same page: the expression of suppressed rage. Defiance feeds on shame. It needs it. Mere defiance will never provide the wherewithal to escape, no matter how much alcohol you pour on its flames, no matter how many achievements you are determined to stack like a tower.

There are commercials for orthodontists now, in which people shake their heads and tell the sad story of having been ashamed to smile, stories in which they can't believe they "waited so long" to get their teeth fixed. This is not one of those stories. I know why I "waited so long." I was broke.

People who have never been poor think poverty is a lack of money. Of course it is that, but worse: poverty is a lack of standing. Being poor means you don't count; you are disregarded, robbed of your dignity, dishonored.

I'd been watching kids' TV with my three year old grandson, probably *Curious George*, or *Shaun the Sheep*, and tickling him, when he threw back his head, laughing, and cracked off one of my front teeth. The tooth had broken below the gum line. There was blood. I looked at the tooth in my palm as I reassured my grandson that he done nothing wrong, that I was fine, but I felt a wave of desperation go over me: I had been invited to a fancy dinner party at a wealthy friend's home. I was going to look like the poor kid in hand-me-downs

I knew I was. I was about to be denied the pretense that I was, or could ever be, anyone else. I had a hole in my face, a grin like a jack-o'-lantern, a vacancy that betokened rot, a signifier of poverty and squalor.

I made an emergency appointment with a dentist known for his problem-solving. He fashioned a tooth, a little sculpture of a tooth really, and affixed it to the edges where my real tooth had broken off. He warned me, as I held the hand mirror he'd given me, that it was precarious and that I needed to be careful what I ate.

My host had invited three others to her table, two of them Pulitzer winners, the other the editor of a major newspaper. She herself had been an ambassador to a European country, a warm, gregarious person whose Christmas parties were legend. The house was a mansion, no other word for it, with a cobbled circular drive, a sculpture garden, and servants, or at least, on this occasion, a private chef. And here, in retrospect, is what I think made it so hard to get myself to write this part: not only is it nearly impossible to write convincingly about feeling shame without feeling it again — the fluttering solar plexus, the hot red ears — I am ashamed, now, to have been so flattered, so craven, such a suck-up.

I hadn't known the reason for the dinner or that I was the guest of honor until it was announced as we were seated at the table, our host holding up my third book of poems and making a toast. I gobbled up their praise like a starving man. Asked to read, I took requests from my host and chose a couple myself. I felt, of course, that I was singing for my supper; that made me feel good, that I'd been invited because of my poems. But it also felt like a kind of audition. I know my host and companions that evening were being generous and sincere in their appreciation. But I was rendered ineligible for enjoyment not only by the worry I would leave a tooth in my dinner roll, but by the social reality: I didn't belong here and nothing could change that, I was acting a part. It wasn't simply that I felt like an imposter, it was more that I'd found my way back to raw shame by seeing the evening as a kind of tryout, a test I had to pass. ("I'm not going to take you anywhere anymore unless you learn how to behave.") I'd been "called up" and didn't want to be "sent down." I had to, literally, keep it together: my tongue carefully testing my fake front tooth all evening. It was a kind of alcohol-free relapse.

Eleanor Roosevelt famously said, "no one can make you feel inferior without your consent." For a while we were treated to that sentiment on billboards, on the sides of buses, in the subway. (I think it was an Apple computer "Think Different" ad campaign but I may be misremembering that.) What I want to explore is the other side of that statement which has always smacked of glibness and "noblesse oblige" to me.

Is there not some victim blaming in that remark? From a certain angle, her assertion can mean that if you feel inferior it's your own fault, you wanted this, you brought this on yourself — charges with which I have been familiar since my childhood encounter with that predatory coach, all statements that grant to people experiencing repeated humiliation an agency they do not have. That perhaps they and their families haven't had for generations. An agency that perhaps they do not even feel they have a right to.

The fact that this statement was made by Eleanor Roosevelt, by all accounts a kind and courageous woman, someone who would not have intended my interpretation, serves to show, particularly alongside the personal kindness of my host and dinner companions, either that I am just too sensitive (more abuser-speak) or that — as I am arguing here — shame is built into the hierarchical organization of all our social relations. One way or another we are all ensorcelled by this paradigm, trapped in the proliferating binary of haves and have nots, of worth and worthlessness, of the powerful and the powerless, of who owns who. Shame is not only a structural feature of our present society, it's a loadbearing wall.

In his blistering brief memoir, *Who Killed My Father*, the French novelist Édouard Louis refuses over and over to inhabit his father's shame; nor is he willing, after his father's death, to go along with the idea that his working class parents' psychic wounds were somehow self-inflicted. Instead, he calls out the abusive and exploitative powers and principalities by name: Prime Minister Jacques Chirac and Health Minister Xavier Bertrand removed dozens of medications from reimbursement by the government's health plan, and Louis, addressing his deceased father says, point-blank: "Jacques Chirac and Xavier Bertrand destroyed your intestines." His father's back was quite literally broken by an accident at work which left him unable to do the heavy labor that had been his job, but in 2009, Prime Minister Nicolas Sarkozy and his accomplice Martin Hersch, perhaps following after Bill Clinton in the U.S., cancelled the stipend he had been receiving, replacing it with a sort of "workfare." Sarkozy scapegoated the vulnerable, the chronically ill, the poor, as freeloaders, "les assistés," winning reelection in the bargain, and Louis doesn't for a moment forgive him. He writes, "This kind of humiliation by the ruling class broke your back all over again." Later, noting his father's late flowering, his love of books and enjoyment of music, he writes, "because of what they've done to your body, you'll never have a chance to uncover the person you've become."

There is hardly any point in enumerating the ways that the ferocious onslaught of twin-party financial capitalism has consumed so much human potential. Over and over it offers only the humiliations of a bogus meritocracy that shames us, while at the same time it invites us to take sole responsibility, and to claim agency, even if only over our own misery. The last thin blanket of dignity is, "It was my own fault."

4

> A man, to be greatly good, must imagine intensely and comprehensively; he must put himself in the place of many others... the great instrument of moral good is the imagination.
>
> — Percy Bysshe Shelley 1821

The only question that interests me now, though, is how we might get free, how we might imagine something better and work toward it. How do we move from shame to defiance and then, ultimately, to *moral imagination*?

And what does it mean, this term "moral imagination?" Is it real? Or only a wish, a hungry child of hope, reaching for a pretty paragraph, settling for a pretty sentence, most of the time having to be content with the phrase itself, holding onto it as a promise, a talisman. I don't mean hope. No, hope is the wrong word, poisoned by history. But I imagine and believe in a jagged hardness that survives, that we are reduced to when we are "up against it" as we say, a toothed wheel that, with its friction against despair, provides the needed spark to kindle possibility. That's what I mean by the term.

After all, what is this dispiriting history of greed, brutality, and conquest to the real history of the world, in relation to the innumerable lives lived to bring us all here? How long is this narrative, really, in the immensity of time?

A jot, an iota, a blip.

If there is such a thing as moral imagination, it only becomes possible with the understanding that there is nothing merely personal, nothing in the world that has only happened to you. I learned this in the most emphatic way when the publication of my memoir *Half The House* led to the arrest and trial of the man who had plunged me so deeply into shame and secrecy and confusion. When he was discovered to have also violated more than 400 other preadolescent boys, I understood that it was not personal. That understanding was a great relief, but I confess to a confusing kind of freefall at the same time. I realized that no matter what I'd been telling myself, some part of me felt like I had participated by virtue of who I was, by how needy I'd been, by my aspirations to be a star. A violation so intimate as childhood rape of course felt personal, but clearly it was not. Abusers always reinforce the perception that it is, and their safety depends upon their victims looking inward for the source of their shame, encouraging anyone not possessed of "power and gold" to "mock themselves and glorify their betters," as Vonnegut put it. Under such pressure the dignity and integrity of both individuals and populations implode.

It seems to me that the only way out of victimhood is clarity about how hierarchical power behaves, always, in every sphere, in every institution, in every situation. And as a writer it's not enough for me to know and recognize "the bully who rules the world" as the late Carol Bly termed him, I have to write against that power. I am often at a loss just what to say, though, beyond what I already understood as a ten-year-old boy: the emperor is naked, but not only that, he's ugly. Here's a short poem I wrote about that emperor:

CAESAR

Arriving at the podium on the tarmac,
he stands up tall and makes a big fuss
rolling up his sleeves like drawing back

his foreskin, and only amnesiacs
still traumatized and children
do not know what happens next.

I refuse the story of the individual instance of violence. I'm just not satisfied with people expressing horror at the abuse of individual children while they pull into the parking lot at Raytheon or Lockheed-Martin to spend the day assembling missiles that will murder schoolchildren in Yemen, Syria, Gaza — other people's children.

In his 1963 essay, "The Artist's Struggle For Integrity" James Baldwin wrote:

> "And what is crucial here is that if it hurt you, that is not what's important. Everybody's hurt. What is important, what corrals you, what bullwhips you, what drives you, torments you, is that you must find some way of using this to connect you with everyone else alive. This is all you have to do it with. You must understand that your pain is trivial except insofar as you can use it to connect to other people's pain; and insofar as you can do that with your pain, you can be released from it, and then

> hopefully it works the other way around too: insofar as I can tell you what it is to suffer, perhaps I can help you to suffer less."

It is all one struggle, the struggle to be free from abusive power — not only from its atrocities, but also from its arrangements, its expectations, its premises.

Hear me out: I'm moved to speak with urgency because I'm an old man and running out of time. I'm a grandparent, not a wild-eyed prophet come to town crying "Repent!" I'm not wearing a sandwich board that says THE END IS NEAR. I can't be with my grandchildren, on the floor with their toys, at the playground, giving them a bath, making a pizza, and hold that view. If I did have such a sandwich board, it might say, IT SEEMS TO ME THAT WE ARE INVITING DISASTER IF WE DON'T EXTRICATE OURSELVES FROM THE WEB OF LIES DESIGNED TO KEEP US STRANGERS TO ONE ANOTHER AND ALIENATED FROM OURSELVES. It would be exhausting carrying around a sandwich board like that!

You could edit it down, though, to something like "We must love one another or die," as W.H. Auden wrote in desperate hope as WWII began. He famously amended that line, even before the war's end, to the stoical "We must love one another *and* die."

Now I read the first, more urgent, less resigned version, to mean that we must find a way out of hatred, political, historical, ancestral, or it will kill all of us. Events since then have shown that when Auden wrote that line, he was prophetic. Maybe to think there can be such a thing as moral imagination or any such way forward is foolishness. I don't know, but there is nothing left for us to do now but search for it.

For Auden, after the deaths of some 80 million presumably loving and lovable people, the whole of his engagement seems to have collapsed into the abyss between those two choices: he renounced the poem entirely and we only have it because his editor included it, with the first version of the line, in Auden's *Collected Poems*.

As the poet Chard deNiord has written, addressing Auden:

> You had forgotten why you wrote the law
> we loved and need to hear in every age.
> It seems that death had turned your mind so purely
> literal that you forgot that we can die
> alive before we die in bed.

I think I understand Auden's despair and why he felt he had to change that conjunction — *Are these the right words? Are they true?* — but I can't help it: When I read those two lines back to back —

> We must love one another or die.
> We must love one another and die.

I feel as if I'm watching, in the space between them, a bombed building crumbling in on itself, representing of course a bombed city, one among many bombed cities — and burning ships, atrocities, death camps, twin mushroom clouds, all of that tragic failure. But now, faced once again with renewed tribal hatreds and feeling the gathering whirlwind, I find the first line more compelling. That first version was an inspired and passionate cry of moral imagination, a prophet's cry: in historical terms, it was a desperate cry, one that went unheeded.

But surely that was not our last chance? That apocalypse in the aftermath of which I have lived my entire life?

5

> "To be a good ancestor is to think beyond two generations, to three, to four, to five and to ten. And we are very bad at that."
>
> — Barry Lopez

I am among the hundreds of thousands of Americans, born just after WWII, whose fathers would likely have been slain in an invasion of Japan, were it not for the atomic bomb. I first heard this fact on television, and struggled to understand it, back when I was ten, the same year I was raped by my coach. I have been compromised, weakened and bewildered, by both these mortifying facts, but I am complicit in neither. Orwell's boyhood insight that *sin could be something that happened to you* and his lifelong refusal to find that acceptable seems essential to the moral imagination. We are not all guilty just because we have been compromised. We are not all equally responsible for the situation we find ourselves in.

I have friends I cherish who hold the view that we as a species are marauders and despoilers. I understand why, but talking about *the human species*, like talking about *human nature*, not only feels wrong to me but smells like the kind of propaganda Gramsci warned us about; it feels like the latest way to normalize the assumptions of an individualist, capitalist, militarist world view. It is a simplistic leveling. A surrender. An excuse: if we are all equally guilty, then none of us are.

We all try to make our separate peace; we must. But it's not, surely it can't be, enough to secure only that. I can't accept that and still believe my love is worth anything when I'm rocking my grandson in my arms, terrified at the world he's arrived in. I might be able to generate hope from the joy my grandchildren give me but that seems unfair. The wildfires burn, the sea encroaches, pandemic is upon us: earth itself appears to be saying that we don't have time for broad descriptors like *the species*, or *human nature*; not unless they are rooted in the vision of something better than this ashen aftermath of terrible mistakes in which live coals are buried.

Dostoyevsky would recognize the place I have come to, where the abuse of a child is at the center of one's understanding of evil, and where moral imagination insists that a real ethical system must be rooted, first and last, in that knowledge. Even if others dismiss it as naïveté:

> I have seen the truth; I have seen and I know that people can be beautiful and happy without losing the power of living on earth. I will not and cannot believe that evil is the normal condition of mankind. And it is just this faith of mine that they laugh at.
>
> — *The Dream of a Ridiculous Man*

Moral imagination is not utopian; it is quite capable of calculus, but before it shrinks from the cost of change, it asks what we are already paying. What is the price of a dimmed life? Of an inhabited delusion mistaken for destiny? We are continually shown the cost if we can bear to look.

Growing up after WWII, my friends and I were always playing war, trying to master a future we imagined from our parents' pasts. We made periscopes from a milk carton and two small cosmetic mirrors so we could see around corners. I think the directions were in the *Cub Scout Handbook*. We'd glue each mirror at a 45° angle in the top and bottom of the carton, taking care to position them correctly, to get the sight-lines right. It was exciting to be able to see around a corner, especially when we were playing some kind of militarized tag, making the sounds of gunfire, pretending to be at war, using our imaginations defensively, adrenalized by a real and abiding terror.

Will I ever look back and not see that milk box jutting out, surveilling me from around a corner in childhood? I doubt it. I can't imagine myself without that boy's fear, his dread and his prayerful hope. Will my frightened grandchildren ever see safety beyond the present? Will they be able, as evidently we cannot, to turn that corner?

Not long ago, my son and daughter got together and bought their parents a "spit kit" from Ancestry.com, a DNA test that confirmed my Northern European genome. I'd wanted a surprise, maybe some forbears less fractious and dour, but the real disappointment was how meaningless and empty the whole inquiry felt afterward.

After all, ancestors are only so useful. There are layers under layers under layers of dead beneath our feet to the very center of the earth, and not one of them can help us. We have only their detritus and their examples, benign and malign, by which to take our bearings. And even then, the examples are mostly speculation, drawn from a militarist history and augmented by fictions — saints and prophets and heroes in whose names, over and over, we make war.

When I went to Europe, it felt familiar. Having been an altar boy, I knew and loved its iconography, its stories, the lore I'd been taught to hold dear. In cathedrals and museums, painting after painting celebrates centuries of bloody conquest, while opposite, the Virgin holds her baby as The Madonna, and also her innocent man-child, despoiled, as The Pietà. Rightly or wrongly, I take the over-arching lesson to be that human life is a binary of war and grief, as if it's the best we can do, the best we can have — a bipolar world that continues making martyrs of any who refuse to submit. Might a future with fewer martyrs be possible?

The first people of that future are already here.

With my grandchildren I laugh for no good reason, laughter that comes in waves, that starts below my feet and passes through me, grounding me. Even at their most exasperating they connect me to life in a way that nothing else can. They teach me what time it is, and who I truly am, lagging behind them out of breath here in our shared present. One day not too far from now they will be my only connection to life.

A few days ago, cleaning up my infant grandson's spilled milk, I thought about the ways he would be cleaning up after me, after my whole generation, long after we're gone. In his diary Dostoyevsky wrote, "The soul is healed by being with children." Yes, but the separate peace of a healed soul is not by itself enough. What is our bequest to these innocent people? I try to post myself where I might know but sometimes it is like standing by a cataract where a stream has been diverted, where it is hard to think above the roar, and hard not to lose heart.

Consider that recently, while I was driving him from basketball practice, my 14-year-old grandson asked me, out of the blue and into the dark silence of the ride home, "if there's a WWIII, I'd do pretty good, right? I think I'd do pretty good. I'm quick and strong. I'm pretty agile, that's what my coach says. If there's a WWIII, I could fight pretty good, don't you think?"

I remembered that the week before, they'd been studying WWI in History class. He was excited that he got a 95 on the quiz. So this week they must have been on to WWII.

Consider that our ancestors dreamed of a thousand years of peace while, here in America, we have never gone a single generation without a war. As I write this, the Russian invasion of Ukraine has begun and the news is filled with urgent voices, towering billows of smoke, sirens, rolling tanks, corpses in the streets, and fleeing people.

Consider that victory in WWIII— a war which already exists as a fearful knot tied in my grandson's imagination — would likely mean living a few days longer than your enemy.

Without an understanding of our bequests, both hopeful and horrifying, I don't see how we can be "good ancestors" of any description. So while I agree with Lopez that we need to be thinking beyond two generations, I would argue also that it is only in those first two generations that we are able to act, change, provide examples. We have no other time in which to oppose a world where a child's purpose is to take part in a mercantile system that creates a market and calls it culture, that places turnstiles in the wilderness, and with that money makes more propaganda for its genocidal and ecocidal arrangements.

Failing to imagine "intensely and comprehensively" is to settle for *Not so bad. Not as bad. At least. It could be worse. Not bad.* Even, idolatrously, *Thank god.* It means to see ourselves as passive victims, our imaginations constrained by a kind of sorcery, consoling ourselves with "'Twas ever thus." But when shame robs us of agency and darkens to dread, we "die/ alive before we die in bed."

We must love one another. Period. And in full knowledge of — but no loyalty to — our ancestors' past failures to do so. We owe that to our descendants.

WHEELS

JUST ACROSS THE STREET from our house, you pick up the bike path to the suburbs west of the city, and my grandson and I often ride on it for about a mile and a half to a cafe in the next town where we rest with a cold drink and a snack before heading back the other way. It's just about the right distance for an eight year old and an old man. Halfway, there is a little park by a pond where we have sometimes fished, where we often stop to sit and talk, or to watch parents and small children throw torn bread to the ducks and Canada geese just as we used to do, back before D became what he calls one of the big kids. Some days we stop there for a long time and just sit by the water, but on this day he's anxious to get back on his bike, not because he has anywhere else to be, but because he has just too much energy coursing through him today to sit on a rock and take turns throwing pebbles with his grandfather.

It may seem strange for a man in his sixties to admire an eight year old boy, but I do. He is a hunter-gatherer of experiences, understandings, meanings, with a kind of curiosity and an attendant integrative power that is, in fact, his careful though unscripted assembly of himself, a continual choosing that makes him more and more a person. I suppose all children who are healthy and protected, and therefore free, are engaged in this process. In any case, I admire the way he has taken what he needs from us, from his parents and grandparents, his friends, his teachers, from the sea-creatures and other animals he loves to read about, from the clouds and stars, from the strangers he's watched and the places he's been. The world is krill to him and as it passes through his mind he extracts its nourishment and grows strong. It may be that other family members, those he does not know because they died before he was born, left him the principles on which he bases his instant to instant decisions about what to take in and what to disregard; in this respect he honors my parents and grandparents and his entire lineage, Black and white, Jamaican and European.

Here I have to unfool myself about what matters and what doesn't: no one in this country can ignore the fact that there is a force-field of white fearfulness into which my grandson moves ever more deeply the older he gets, and I can't fool myself that we, on both sides of his family, will be able to spare him very much of that, for all our love. Even in our city — Cambridge, Massachusetts, supposed bastion of progressive values — I can recall white parents on occasion directing their little playground rats away from him until I speak to him; then they would flash me a wan smile meant, I guess, to deny their motive. Or maybe it expresses their chagrin at not having noticed that the boy was with me, the white guy who presumably makes it all right for this Black boy to be there.

We slot our bikes into the rack and hang our helmets on the handlebars. The cafe's crowded and there's a line to the counter. At a table nearby, a teenage boy in a wheelchair is being fed through a straw by a woman who looks to be his mother. I recognize the round face, the narrow shoulders, the lolling head of someone with Duchenne muscular dystrophy, the disease that killed my brothers Bobby and Mike. The boy raises a hand and it flops to the side of the chair. His mother replaces it on his tray. The way he struggles to lift his head to look back and up at his mother behind his wheelchair twists something loose inside me, a memory: pushing my brother's wheelchair, attending him, coming around front when I note him struggling to turn to me. The boy's mother comes around and kneels in front of him, and I feel my brother Bobby's presence as I have not for a long time.

We grew up together, a year apart, sometimes mistaken for twins, and it wasn't until he was just about D's age that his illness began to separate us, when he couldn't keep up, when more and more often he fell behind or simply fell. In a way, Bobby has remained with me through the decades since his death, most often as a vague pull, a necessity to describe or explain things, a habit I developed as I rode my bicycle farther and farther from home, returning to him in his wheelchair with whatever stories, observations, experiences I'd gathered. Still, there are certain times when he feels present to me, when he is even after all these years right here with me, as if I am once again pushing his chair, and I almost want to bend forward to hear him.

D is staring at the boy. I distract him with a shoulder squeeze, "Hey, focus now. What do you want to eat?" He can't help himself, he turns to look back at the boy. Then he turns to me and, mimicking the boy's movements, asks in a whisper, "What's wrong with that kid?"

I'm surprised by the wave of anger that washes over me then. I suppose it is a kind of memory, this emotion. I used to get furious at people who stared at my brother as if he was not my brother whose muscles were betraying him but something altogether different, as if he was something wrong — sometimes I'd snap at them, "Take a picture!"

And then it really is as if my brother is right there with me. "*Easy,*" he says, just as he used to. I was always more upset by people's stares than he was. *Easy.* And then more often than not he would say hello to the person who'd been staring at him, requiring a response from them, turning himself from object to subject. Still, I can't entirely get the edge off my voice when I say to D, "Don't do that. He might think you're making fun of him."

"But I wasn't," D insists in a loud whisper, "I wasn't making fun of him!"

"I know, D. I know you weren't. Let's order."

He steals another look at the boy, whose mother is pushing him toward the exit. A man puts down his newspaper and helps with the door. We take our chips and sodas to a table by the window.

We don't seem to be able to leave the moment behind; it hangs between us, so I decide to tell D the story of my brother. I don't mention my younger brother Mike, dead of the same illness, and I tell him a version of the story that I hope is suited to his eight year-old's understanding. If I remember correctly, it went something like this:

"That boy who was here in the wheelchair? He was sick with an illness called muscular dystrophy. I know because my brother, Bobby, had it. It makes your muscles weaker and weaker so you can't do the things you used to be able to do, like run or ride your bike, or even walk after a while. Even the muscles that hold you up straight or help you hold up your head get weak." D pulls his legs up so his feet are on the chair with him, his chin on his knees. "He would have been your grand uncle."

I can see that I have to explain what I mean by grand "Because I'm your grandfather, my brother would be called your grand uncle."

"Oh."

"He was really smart, especially at math. And he read lots of books. He loved watching baseball on TV and keeping score of all the games."

"Wait," D says. "Did he *die*?"

And he says the word "die" as if it might mean fly to the moon or sink to the bottom of the sea.

"Yes." I think there must be more to say, but I don't know what it is. I busy myself with pulling apart the top of the bag of chips. "You want me to open yours? Can you get it?"

D shakes his head, taking it as a challenge, and deftly pulls open the bag along the seal. He puts a large intact chip in his mouth. "You like seafood?"

"No!" I laugh and turn away. That's when I notice the man a couple of tables from us abruptly turn his head away. I feel sure he's been staring at us.

When I was a boy, I used to ride my bike to the library and bring home books for Bobby, mostly biographies of athletes and books of American history. I cannot keep the chronology straight: it seems now that right about the time his wheelchair became a constant feature of Bobby's life, right around D's age now, my bicycle became a constant part of mine. My bike took me away from home, away from my brother, into an exhilarating freedom. I rode my bike to the park, to the creek, to the other side of town. I rode to my friends' houses, rode to the store for my mother, rode to the library. And into danger. Not only from cars, but from the sexual predations of adults as well. "Come here, kid. Come here. I won't hurtcha...." Although it is true that most kids are abused by someone they know, in my own case a baseball coach, it's also true that those threats were everywhere; besides, I rode my bike to baseball practice.

I got the bicycle. Bobby got the wheelchair.

My brother is alive in me as a habit of mind, by virtue of my collecting things to bring him, by my thinking about what would amuse or delight him. No doubt this began with those trips uptown to the library, but later my hunting and gathering took the form of selecting from my experiences of the day — the ballgame, the movie, the funny, stupid, or sometimes interesting things I heard people say as I rode my bike through the streets and alleys and parks.

When Bob died, it was as if our roles were suddenly reversed, as if, for the first time, he had bested me: I was always the one who did things that he couldn't. It was less a competition between us, though, than a goad. One of us had to do for both of us, but that had always been me, the active one. When he died, along with my grief and my anger at the unfairness of his life, I felt that he had done something amazing. Now it seems to me a strange, perhaps perverse, morbid, and self-centered view.

"I need to go to the bathroom," D says.

"You know where it is, right?" He nods. As soon as he is around the corner to the restrooms, the man who has been watching us gets up and moves toward the mens' room. I can almost hear Bobby again, *Easy.* But he doesn't know the things I know, the things I learned, free in the world on my bicycle. I recall that the bathroom's a one-seater and I'm relieved to see the man waiting outside, leaning against the wall. I pretend to read the notices and business cards on the community bulletin board in the hallway until D comes out. Then I go back to the table with him. I want the man to know he was noticed.

"Finish your drink," I say, "It's time to get going." I drain my bottle of Orangina.

Outside, we get our bikes from the rack, fasten our helmets, start out. "It feels like rain," I say. I can feel it in my knees, neck, and lower back.

D passes me, whooping. He tries to pop a wheelie. I pedal along in my geriatric way, feeling heavy. I'm still thinking of my brother who flew to the moon, who sank to the bottom of the sea.

"Grandpa, c'mon!" D yells back over his shoulder. He wants me to catch up.

FROM THE DEPTHS

NOW, WHEN PHOTOS OF neo-Nazis, of White Nationalists, appear again and again in the newspaper, on social media, on TV, I find myself looking for a certain face among them, looking again and again at the pixelated faces of hatred, white men carrying torches, chanting slogans, brandishing weapons, storming the Capitol. In a kind of angry and fearful version of "Where's Waldo?" I am looking for Andrei.

A dozen years ago, Andrei, whose name is not Andrei, had approached me at a 12-step meeting and asked if I would be willing to help him. He was hollow-eyed, dirty, biting at his cuticles, his face and nose scraped bloody. I offered to buy him a cup of coffee and talk. For whatever reason, this seemed to throw him into a panic, "No, no, I mean thank you, but could I just have your phone number so I can call you?"

We spoke regularly for about six months, Andrei getting visibly better, sometimes even smiling. We were both attending a meeting where the group works through one of the 12 steps each week. Often we talked on the sidewalk outside, where he would hang out with the other smokers. I learned from him that he had been hospitalized for depression, that he'd been kicked out of a group home for drinking, that he was angry at the state mental health system. Once he'd reestablished his abstinence, and agreed to take his medications, he was allowed to return.

It was months before we shared a laugh, when, at the mid-meeting break, an avalanche of snow came down off the roof on a guy trying to light a cigarette. I remember because as I laughed, I touched my hand to his shoulder a moment and he recoiled almost violently. I made a mental note not to touch him again.

Andrei was estranged from his parents, and told me that he could now see how badly he had let them down. He was especially remorseful about the way he had treated his father the last time he'd seen him. "Richard, I really abused the man. I mean, the guy's doing his best. He came here from Russia, hardly speaks any English even now. When I was growing up the other kids made fun of him and I would get my ass kicked trying to stick up for him. Sticking up for myself, I guess. Richard, I rejected him. I told him he was a fucking loser. What kind of a son does that? What kind of a person? I broke his heart."

We were coming to Step 9: *Made direct amends to such people wherever possible, except when to do so would injure them or others*, and soon after that, Andrei the prodigal son paid his father a visit in Florida. He wept when he told me about it. "We were bawling our eyes out. He was so happy to see me! Why was he happy to see me? Why? After all I'd said and done, all the hurt I caused him?"

He wanted to go to art school, or to study art history. After his second year of continuous sobriety, he made me a book in which he mounted reproductions of his favorite Rembrandt paintings on colored paper, hand lettering information from art history texts on each page, sewing it together with colored thread and ribbon. It was a beautiful one-of-a-kind gift I still have.

Andrei continued to put his life back together. He moved into his own place. He found a job he liked, with people he enjoyed. Our conversations changed. We talked about recovery, of course, about what alcohol had done for us, and then to us, its outsized place in our lives. I remember telling him that clarity was the virtue I valued most because I had fooled myself so many times. I don't recall the context of that conversation, but remember I meant it as a gentle admonishment in response to something he'd said. I told him something of my life. I showed him pictures of my beloved grandson, my daughter's boy, whose Jamaican father was just then in prison. I talked about my father, who was dying. We were becoming friends. He was working full-time, and now that he had a little money, he began to invite me for lunch, always insistent that he would pay.

At one point, when I had not seen him for a couple of months, I arrived to meet him in a cafe and hardly recognized him. He had lost a good deal of weight; he was in great shape, smartly dressed, and with a vitality I had never seen in him before. I told him he looked great. He told me he had gone off his medications.

"It's dope is what it is. I've been so doped up for so long I haven't been able to feel a thing. To stay in the group home I had to take the meds they gave me. Turned me into a fucking zombie. I'm done with all that." He'd met a woman he called his girlfriend. "You want anything else? No, no, sit. I'll get it. Ice tea? A napkin? Remember this is on me."

Then, about two weeks later I came home late to a message. "Richard. Yeah. This is Andrei. Listen, I just wanted to tell you that I'm going to get drunk tonight. I decided... you know what just fuck it. I just figured I owe it to you to let you know, man. That's all. That's it." I called him. No answer. First thing in the morning I called again.

"Nah. I changed my mind," he said. "I just went to sleep. Finally." It turned out his girlfriend, a coworker, had thought he just wanted to be friends, and she'd rejected him as anything more than that. She was a college student. Andrei was in his fifties. Their romance had been largely in his head.

"Listen, I think you need some help, Andrei. You know what I mean? Not just the Steps."

"So they can dope me up again? No fucking way, man."

"No, no. Not the state system. I'm not talking about that. What if I found you a referral? You've got insurance right? Somebody who could just sit with you and help you sort things out. You wouldn't have to take any meds. Not like that."

"I guess you're right."

So I made some calls to therapist friends, came up with a name. We'll call him Mark Silver. Andrei thanked me and said he would continue to let me know how he was doing. A month later, having heard nothing from him, and not having seen him at a meeting, I came home from teaching an evening class to a voicemail from him:

> *Richard. OK. Here goes — I'm not going to sit in a small airless room and talk about my miserable emasculated white male life and what a fucking loser I am while all the fucking castrated feminized males like you with all your liberal bullshit are getting laid because you sold out to the feminazi bitches who have your balls in a vice, man. So as for your so-called help, no fucking thank you, OK? I'm a Eurocentric white man and proud of it. I know you*

*went to Latin America last summer, and man they pulled the wool over your eyes good. Those ni**ers showed you just what they wanted you to see so you'd look the other way while they go on to ni**erize the world and stupid liberals like you think they're so primitive and cute. You need to wake the fuck up, man. The ni**ers already got your daughter, man, and knocked her up and took your money and betrayed you. I know you think that ni**er's gone, in prison for a long time, but you just wait: some Radcliffe cunt who's already sucking his dick will get him out and then he'll be back to fuck you over again. And another thing: that guy you sent me to is a Jew. Oh boo fucking hoo for the poor victims of the phony holocaust. Poor poor Jews who are committing genocide and I don't care if that's politically incorrect. You tell me I should try to meet a woman my own age but they're all emasculating cunts, man, and if you don't have any money they're not interested. They only want to fuck if they get paid. A bunch of whores. When are you going to wake the fuck up, man, and be white and quit bending over begging for that black ni**er cock up your ass?* BEEP. To hear this message again press 1, to save it press 2, to erase it press 3. To forward this message press 4.

I stood there next to my desk shaking as rage coursed through me: wordless, white-hot, I-will-kill-you rage. I remember the smell of me then: fear, metallic and rank, so much so that after I put down the phone and took a long hot shower, I still smelled it when I returned to that room. Although it was January, I opened all the windows.

But the tears rolling down my cheeks were grief, too: I had just heard a man crying out from hell. He desired nothing more than to share his agony with all those he believed had cheated him and injured him. I wonder if that desire is not itself the definition of hell. I wanted to call him back, rage back at him, roar at him, put all that ugliness I wasn't able to wash off back on him.

And there was the voicemail. Not only did I not want to hear it again, I wanted it gone. I pressed 3. As it turns out, a recording would have been redundant: every syllable of that utterance is seared in my memory, and I don't know how to delete it.

It's true, of course, that Andrei was deeply, severely mentally ill, and in the midst of some kind of episode. But that's also a dodge. Our culture offers the menu of perennial scapegoats he chose; he didn't invent them. And his message could not have been more articulate; there was no stammering, no searching for the right word. His monologue was rapid and efficient. It sounded practiced, as if he had written it out ahead of time. ("OK. Here goes —"?) Had he rehearsed his message? Read it aloud to himself before he called? Is racism a pathology? Is misogyny a sickness? Antisemitism a disease? Is hate? What is evil?

For weeks after that message I was in shock, walking around with an emptiness in the pit of my stomach and a mind full of loose threads as if something had been violently torn from it. I did nothing; it was not a decision, it's just what I did — nothing. Should I have called him back him back? Argued with him? Called the police to alert them to a psychopath who was — what? — making hateful telephone calls? I only wanted him to keep his distance, far from me and my family. I left his message inside a sort of parenthesis for 12 years, a blister or pustule I chose to ignore until now.

I have never fully accepted that people can be at once inspiring and courageous and also vicious and malign. I have always known this of course; who hasn't learned this in childhood? But knowing and accepting are not the same thing. I still find this twinned capacity for beauty and cruelty a paradox that grinds against hope: cold sparks of irony shoot out and, igniting neither action nor idea, leave me enervated and sadder than I already was.

What the hell had I been telling myself about Andrei? Was my whole experience of him a fiction he'd offered me? I had certainly suspended disbelief. Had I co-authored his story, our story, this story? Was he manipulating me, playing me for his advantage? Of what use to me, to my idea of myself, was he? Were we both reading from an inherited script while busily denying it to ourselves?

These are not even the most important questions but because there is a better chance I might be able to say something useful by asking them, I'll take them up first.

The story I was telling myself about Andrei both was and was not a fiction, just as the story he told me of a ne'er-do-well, black sheep, fuck-up, loser was both true and not. My version was derived, at least most immediately, from my own recovery and from having seen a couple of decades worth of people regain their dignity, hope, and self-respect, and go on to remake their lives. In my version, informed by my own experience, addicts were trauma survivors who had developed a persona to hide behind. Sometimes it was a hard-drinking world-beater, other times it was a cringing pitiable wreck begging *Don't hurt me, please.* Somewhere there was a violated innocence which meant, at least to me, that there was an innocence that might be reclaimed, a capacity for delight, for laughter and kindness, for friendship and connection. I had experienced this in my own life, and I had witnessed it in others' many times.

So, for me, Andrei's explosion of hatred and contempt represented a crisis of faith, a challenge, and also a terror —

that I could never truly know anyone, only my filtered, subjective impression of them. Something the great Portuguese poet Fernando Pessoa wrote of with more acceptance than I:

> We are our dreams of ourselves, souls by gleams,
> And each to each other dreams of others' dreams.

I told myself that I believed in openness, in candor as a disarming strategy, a way across difference, a bridge. Was I a fool? And moreso now if I still think so? Maybe in addition to foolishness, my confidence in people's good intentions is laziness. Maybe I hate exercising good judgment as much as I hate exercise. In any case, I've always been this way. I think that nearly everyone is doing the best they can, that Lucinda Williams is right when she sings (quoting a poem by her father Miller Williams), "You do not know/what wars are going on/down there where the spirit meets the bone." That Thomas à Kempis is correct: "Be assured that if you knew all, you would pardon all." But maybe what I tell myself is compassion is really a dodge; suspending judgment precludes most actions, lets me off the hook. Maybe like everyone else, I'm doing the best I can.

The real terror is not that I misread Andrei, but that I could be so ignorant of who I am, that my dream of myself was so far off the mark. I'd been telling myself I had something to do with Andrei's recovery, that my encouragement and witness were valuable. That felt good. When after a year or so his attendance at meetings dropped off, I told myself that everyone recovers differently, that he was best able to judge what he needed. I wasn't about to ride herd on him. I never, ever, gave him direct advice. I already knew how that would turn out; in fact, that should have been my first warning, that he complained to me, angrily, about how rigid his earlier sponsors had been.

Even after more than a year of AA meetings and coffees with me weekly, usually in the same booth in the same diner, Andrei had a hard time making eye contact. I thought this was residual shame for having been the ragged and broken man I first met, grimy, bloodied, and smelling like a week's worth of piss. I tried to talk to him as if he were already a whole person, but I always remembered how he looked that first day. From the start I saw him as more sinned against than sinning, as a man who had fallen among thieves. I didn't know who the thieves were, other than alcohol and drugs, only that they had taken everything and beaten him nearly to death. For whatever reason, he had arrived at mid-life ill-equipped to meet its demands. I felt sympathy for the soul I saw "by gleams," the soul that in our age is hard to know how to care for: Every birth is among ruins of some kind, a junk-dealer's yard, an archive with a jumbled index. It seemed simple to me: the best way to support someone seeking respectability was to respect them.

By my anecdotes about work and family and friends, by sharing my own frustrations and failures, by modeling a relaxed honesty, I tried to disarm his suspicious nature and invite a reciprocal candor. I told myself that even if that was a little manipulative, if my interactions with Andrei were a bit studied (as much as I tried to disguise that fact) it was all for his benefit, all part of the rescue effort.

Ah, there we have it — rescue. I didn't really believe I was rescuing him though; it wasn't that cut and dried. It was more that I was caught up in a trope that made me feel good. I was a lousy sponsor, with lousy boundaries, and once Andrei began to improve, he slowly and subtly became a personal project. As he cleared up, from both alcohol and the many colliding medications he'd been prescribed, he must have seen the disproportion between our lives, and took my refusal to acknowledge it for the patronizing that, on some level, I suppose it was.

That patronizing was at least partly what kept me from understanding who he really was. At our standing date for coffee on Sundays, I often showed him pictures of my grandson — on my wife's knee, in my daughter's arms, in his father's lap, taking his first steps — until one Sunday I finally noticed how uncomfortable I was making him. I stopped then, changed the subject — what the hell was I doing reveling in the love of family, of children and grandchildren, to a guy alone, in his 50s, struggling still to get a foothold, a car, a job. I hadn't meant to be cruel. I almost asked him for forgiveness, but I couldn't figure out how without making things worse. But I had been even more oblivious than I thought: I completely missed it, the racism, the fact that his squirming and grimacing was not about my being insensitive, but about my grandson's race.

I should have seen it. Why I didn't is an important question to take up.

When I look again at the handmade book of reproductions he made as a gift for me, I see that he was deeply entranced by Europe, but his Europe was the one James Baldwin encountered in his essay "Stranger in the Village," a place where there are not and have never been any people other than white Europeans, and certainly no Black people. That is my most charitable interpretation, though; more charitable than his phone message deserves. He urged CDs on me by bands called *Peste Noire, Absurd, Screwdriver, Odin's Law, Prussian Blue.* I took them home but didn't listen to them. I'd never had any use for Heavy Metal. I was stuck in my tastes in popular music: Blues, Jazz, Classical. When he asked me if I'd listened to the music he lent me, I lied, and when he asked me what I thought, I just said it wasn't my thing. Recently I looked up these bands and found they're grouped under the heading "National Socialist Black Metal" — neo-Nazi music.

I had no idea 12 years ago that there was such a movement. My parents' generation had so roundly defeated Nazism that to me Nazis were merely emblems of a vanquished evil. Or they persisted as objects of derision and laughter, cartoonish characters in comedies like *Hogan's Heroes*, and Indiana Jones movies. A full-on commitment to Nazism, to white nationalism, so far as I knew, was the province of a few Neanderthal idiots in isolated pockets of the country. Now I can't help but wonder if today's reemergence of Nazism, abetted by cynical grifters and opportunist demagogues, is the result of the same kind of denial, patronizing, and self-involvement on the part of my countrymen that I'm accusing myself of in relation to Andrei? Maybe our relationship was a microcosm; maybe we were in different boats on the same tide. Anyway, it's a recognizable dynamic: the reluctance to see malevolence so long as you're getting what you need: the assurance that you are a good person, and that you are just fine thank you very much. I thought I was doing something good. I thought I was helping Andrei learn how to be at ease with himself. I'd hoped he would make his way to his real questions and quit punishing himself, quit being ashamed. Back then I believed that questions about self-worth were never the right ones. For anyone. There are people who don't recover from trauma, or who don't recover from their addiction, because they don't believe they deserve to. Now I wonder if I was wrong. I don't know what Andrei was ashamed of, but any man who could leave a phone message vile as his, mentally ill or not, is capable of doing, or of having done, almost anything. Maybe that's the hell I heard him curse me from, into which he was cast by his own conscience.

I don't know, and only here, where I have disguised his identity, do I feel I dare speculate. What if, in Andrei's case, spirits were the spirit who restrained him? What if his alcoholism was the best part of him, desperately holding him back from expressing his rage and hatred, mercifully incapacitating him? What if his alcoholism was the only constraint left? What if his addiction was his conscience speaking?

I said I would first take up the questions I might find answers to, but with the exception of seeing that I was a fool, that my naïvetè and self-soothing idealism were dangerous, I haven't come up with much, only more questions. Now when I think back on the last time we met, when he bought me lunch, when he told me he'd gone off his meds, I remember how manic he seemed, and how I kept smiling at him calmly, trying to be supportive. Christ, it was like Don Quixote comforting Faust, Pangloss offering Raskolnikov a fresh start.

I can sneer at myself as well as the next guy, maybe better, but when all is said and done I believe in hope. I don't know how else to engage with people; without hope, most people just aren't worth it. To be honest, I believe people's behavior is more often driven by fear of punishment than by conscience.

There have always been thugs and rapists, night riders, pogroms and lynchings, not to mention those who bomb the homes of others, destroy their crops, poison the water, murder, dig mass graves, and then raise statues to commemorate their conquests, legitimize their crimes, and establish themselves as the powers and principalities of the world. How do they bring themselves to do these things? What is life to them? Do they think they know what life is? I don't. And if they are right I don't want to.

There have been betrayals and disappointments, of course, but every bit of love I ever received was a response to my hope. When I engaged with people in fear and in shame, I was left with ashes.

What sort of tropism is this abiding hope that it doesn't seek consolation, that it holds out for joy? Less a resistance to uncertainty than a trust in it, it is a trust in time itself, in the wobble of the planet as it spins. This kind of hope is a question, one we inherit, an orientation of the self, not a wish for a particular outcome.

I have it from my parents, for whom it was a daily requirement, and especially from my mother — it is therefore religious; after all, what is more religious than a mode of being you inherit from your mother? It is larger than — but includes — my Catholic education, along with my boyhood of terror and violent abuse. A part of me is still a boy in his bed in the Cold War dark, terrified and mumbling the rosary for world peace, the droning whisper like a prayer flag in a constant wind. And a part of me is even now reassuring me that my mother's hope was not unreal. It sustained her (and all of us); it opposed, courageously, the hopelessness of two dying children. And so, a survivor, I am a child of that hope, and I seem to do first whatever it takes to protect hope's tender heart. I don't know what resources my mother drew on; I am drawing on hers.

I had never been to Germany, my great-grandparents' country. I had a friend there, in Nuremberg, and she arranged for me to give a reading and a lecture at Johannes Gutenberg University of Mainz so I could get the college where I was teaching to foot the bill for the trip. My wife and I flew into Frankfürt, a gleaming glass city rebuilt after World War II. One of the first things we noticed, walking from the train station to our hotel, was a sculpture dedicated to the victims of the Holocaust. Carved from stone, twisted bodies in agony seemed to be praying, clearly to no avail. Along with other monuments, memorials, and museums throughout Germany and Austria, it seemed a penitent acknowledgment of the darkest moment in Europe's history. My wife and I thought the same thing at the same time: where is there such penitent admission of historical atrocities in U.S. cities? After a nap to relieve our jet lag, we headed for the old city. I wanted some romance, not steel and glass.

The Römerberg is the central cobbled square of the Altstadt, the oldest part of the city, its architecture dating to the Middle Ages. I fell into a dream looking at the half-timbered houses with their graduated roof lines, their plaster and wattle, their balconies of flowering plants, their Romanesque turrets. My first attempt to speak my great-grandparents' native tongue was to order *Schweinebraten mit Sauerkraut und Knödel* in a restaurant there. This was my father's favorite dish, made for him each year on his birthday, first by his mother, then by mine. The pork was delicious, the sauerkraut golden and hot, the dumpling the perfect texture. I looked out onto the square with its colorful array of merchant carts (it was market day), no cars, no trolleys, and for a moment I touched something I knew from my German Catholic boyhood, an aesthetic experience made up of all that my grandparents had been raised to revere, the Old Country: gothic calligraphy on the restaurant menu and on the wooden fascia above its entrance, the carved lintels, the heavy doors with their massive iron hinges. I half expected a Teutonic knight on horseback to come clopping into the square; I imagined my genes were singing as I savored the sweet fat of the *Schweinefleisch.*

The next day we took the train to Nuremberg to visit my friend, a painter and photographer whose family has lived there for generations, a woman whose parents were members of the Nazi party. For her, I know, the past is not safely in the realm of fantasy, and her anger at her parents' hateful politics has animated her life as an artist and Buddhist peace activist. Soon after we arrived, she showed us around a bit to orient us. We stood in the *Hauptmarkt*, another broad cobbled square of medieval buildings, looking up at the ornate mechanical clock on the western face of the Church of Our Lady where, at noon, after the ringing of the church bells, carved trumpeters and drummers come to life, and doors open on either side of the seated figure of Charles IV dressed in gold. A procession of carved and painted puppets, the seven electors who chose Charles IV as the Holy Roman Emperor, pass by him carrying symbols of their offices and their fealty. They have been doing so for more than 600 years.

We had coffee in a little outdoor cafe on a corner of the *Hauptmarkt*; I remember sitting there and thinking it was lovely, this old world, where attention was paid to beauty, where steel, glass, and price per cubic meter hadn't reduced the world to a ledger.

My friend thought we should see the Documentation Center, a museum on the grounds of the 1930s Nazi Party Rally Grounds, but she felt no need to accompany us there. Nuremberg's history was alive for her and painful. "Fascination and Terror," the Center's devastating permanent exhibit, traces the factors that gave rise to Nazism, the ways that the Party normalized its cult of hatred, spread its propaganda, and appealed to a demoralized and resentful German population. The exhibition was moving and not a little frightening. Nazism was rooted in centuries of antisemitism, and room after room, moving forward in time from the early Middle Ages to the 20th century, exposed the deep rhizome of hatred from which, whenever conditions were right, murderous pogroms sprouted. I was struck by the juxtaposition of two images. The first a medieval painting of serene blonde angels with swords driving grimacing swarthy demons into a pit, and the other a black and white photo of SS troops armed with rifles and submachine guns in the act of similarly prodding Jews to the edge of a mass grave, already half-filled. It was there that I learned that the Romanesque church that had so enchanted me, the *Frauenkirche*, was built on the site of a synagogue burned to the ground during the pogrom of 1349, which followed an outbreak of The Black Plague. Charles IV erected it to "Our Lady" and was crowned Holy Roman Emperor there, the scene commemorated on its ingenious clock. And I remember my shock when, in an enlarged still from Leni Riefenstahl's *Triumph of the Will*, crowds marched with Nazi banners, torches and swastikas down the street where I recognized the same cafe on the same corner where I had earlier indulged my fantasy of a pre-industrial market town. So much for ancestral nostalgia.

And so much for Nazis: my aesthetic sweet spot was theirs as well, and they evangelized its beauty, from Goethe and Heine to Bach, Beethoven, and Strauss, down to the last dirndl and lederhosen and beerfest of the *Herrenvölk*, all the while worshipping death and calling it purity.

So, I believe I understand something of Andrei's Europhilia, but also its dark turn toward *Lebensraum*. And, even though I know it is reductionist and simplistic, I can't help wondering at the value of a culture that, for all its beauty, regularly erupts in genocidal violence.

Over and over, I'd felt the weight of the past, the heft of it, its substance, in a way that is impossible in America. Not only are we a "young country," but we only barely acknowledge the circumstances of our being here: genocide on a continental scale and the capture and breeding of human beings for profit. As I write this, today's Nazis, America's Nazis, are purging school curricula of references to those two foundational facts, persecuting teachers, terrorizing school boards, banning books and films that even mention them. When you live inside a myth, denying history, the past is a theme park. Also a desiccation, a petrifaction, a metaphysical necrophilia. Nostalgia wafting from it like a poison gas.

No vile ideology is without allies. Destructive ideas have much in common despite their differences. Vultures, hyenas, voles, worms, and maggots don't need to conspire to pick a carcass clean.

Certain things seem occultly bound to other things, certain attitudes seem to have formed a root system in the same darkness. White supremacy is aligned with male supremacy everywhere, and the fundamentalist versions of otherwise warring religions all agree on male supremacy as the primary principle of their envisioned future, including the bedrock idea that masculine dishonor must be met with righteous corrective violence.

Andrei's mental illness does not explain his choice of targets; he chose them from a menu that seems never to change: women, Jews, nonwhite people, and those, like me, who remain benighted and do not realize the need to fight back against these "enemies."

It even seems to me possible that Andrei's mental illness did not precede his encounter with this list of targets, but in fact grew from the broader culture of misogyny, racism, and antisemitism, grew from it as if it had been cultivated in a petri dish. (I use the word culture the way a high school biology teacher might explain it, as a place where conditions allow some organisms to grow and spread while others cannot.) Andrei's pain was real, his words were political. He believed it was his pain that was political, an oppression, and that his response was natural, justified, even somehow righteous and revolutionary.

I had never heard the term "incel" until recently, and from conversations with others I suspect that there are still many people unfamiliar with it. The term originated on a website meant to provide support to men and women who were involuntarily celibate. Soon, however, "men's rights" organizations flooded the site's conversations and brought along all their ideological cousins, politicizing and martialing cadres of lonely men. After that, the resentments proliferated, various allied groups coming aboard, until a hateful and violent victim identity became the norm.

In 2014, Elliot Rodger, a hero to this new movement of straight men calling themselves "incels," opened fire at a sorority house at University of California, Santa Barbara. Unable to get inside the sorority, he opened fire on a sidewalk of pedestrians, killing six people, then turned the gun on himself, becoming a martyr: incels hate women so much that they now have a term for mass murder followed by suicide: "going all ER on them."

I don't know for certain that Andrei identified with this movement, but his message to me is certainly animated by the same assumptions: that men have a right to women's bodies, that white European civilization is under attack, that people of color are plotting white genocide. His actual affiliation doesn't matter to me; I am trying to grasp what it is that turns suffering into grievance and then into a twisted ideology of violent retribution. That sexual frustration must turn into violence is a simplistic trope that relies on a sort of hydraulic theory of male sexuality: the pressure of celibacy builds until it must explode in violent, perhaps ecstatic, release. I find this idea as insulting to men as the incel's trope of phallic entitlement is destructive to women.

Andrei didn't see people, I know that much. Men were superiors, inferiors, or fools; women were, well, pussy. Andrei never knew a woman, in any sense of that verb. But I don't believe he ever knew a man either, not really. People to Andrei seem to have been all pronouns and body parts, their worth determined by their place in a racial and gender hierarchy. Unable to connect on any level more subtle or complex than the imagined solidarity of the aggrieved, his isolation was complete.

Each of his hatreds, the usual interconnected phobias and bigotries, has a low-grade, chronic form that is widespread and still largely unquestioned. Misogyny is in the air men breathe when together. You hear it in the clubhouse, at the bar, in the locker room, at the poker game, in the box seats and in the bleachers, in jokes and anecdotes and stories, in that punch on the arm, that wink, that smirk. Men showing their disdain for women and insisting to one another, with more than a touch of homophobia, that they love pussy. Can you deny it? It's Manhood 101. Andrei got an A+ in the course. Most men get a "Gentleman's C," having gone along to get along, and profess outrage at attitudes like Andrei's. Often it seems that the anger is really at the naked expression of hatred, not the hatred itself. It is painful to say it, but I grew up in a liberal-minded working-class family who believed they were not racists because they shrank, mostly, from using the n -word, were polite, and tipped the Black bathroom attendant at the fairgrounds.

As a part of the larger backlash, incels believe they are rising to the defense of a civilizational identity besieged by women and people of color. Arch conservatives, they align themselves with a fundamentalism — Christian, Hindu, Jewish, Muslim, it doesn't matter — that hides its misogyny (though not very well) in rituals, rites, liturgies, and rules, the essence of its various doctrines the same male supremacy.

There is more than the use of a gun uniting the killing of worshippers at Mother Emanuel and Tree of Life; more than the fact of an AR-15 connecting these murders to Pulse and Parkland, Tops supermarket and the Atlanta spas.

But the attempt to understand this plaited knot of hatred, as if it were part of a philosophical conversation, merely, is beside the point, as if one day we will solve the problem, understand evil, and then set everything to rights. Ha. Where would we have to stand to gain that kind of vantage? Too often we confuse verbosity with intelligence, passivity with a sage worldliness, and doing nothing with taking the high road.

Is racism a pathology? Shall we convene a symposium on it? Here's the thing: it isn't a conversation. The history of racism, misogyny, antisemitism, is a bellowing voice drowning out any other discourse, or a roaring cascade that remains a part of our interactions, no matter what still waters whiteness leadeth us beside. It's not a conversation, it's a struggle. For some it is a struggle for breath itself.

George Floyd was not having a conversation with Derek Chauvin although he did speak to him: "Oh lord, oh lord, please don't kill me," is what he said. Rayshard Brooks, the long video of his pleading exchange with his killer notwithstanding, did not "converse" with the police. Philando Castile tried to have a conversation with the officer who shot him seated in his girlfriend's car, with her beside him and her 5-year-old in the backseat. And on and on and on.

And back and back and back:

> Mr. Gore once undertook to whip one of Colonel Lloyd's slaves, by the name of Demby. He had given Demby but few stripes, when, to get rid of the scourging, he ran and plunged himself into a creek, and stood there at the depth of his shoulders, refusing to come out. Mr. Gore told him that he would give him three calls, and that, if he did not come out at the third call, he would shoot him. The first call was given. Demby made no response, but stood his ground. The second and third calls were given with the same result. Mr. Gore then, without consultation or deliberation with any one, not

> even giving Demby an additional call, raised his musket to his face, taking deadly aim at his standing victim, and in an instant poor Demby was no more. His mangled body sank out of sight, and blood and brains marked the water where he had stood.

This is from Frederick Douglass's *Narrative of the Life of Frederick Douglass, an American Slave,* published in 1845, 177 years ago. He goes on to tell us about several other such murders and the total indemnity of the white murderers.

Mr. Gore's defence —

> He argued that if one slave refused to be corrected, and escaped with his life, the other slaves would soon copy the example; the result of which would be the freedom of the slaves, and the enslavement of the whites. Mr. Gore's defence was satisfactory.

— is nearly precisely the position of Great Replacement fear-mongers and White Nationalists today. Recently, Donald Trump, then President of the United States, angered by Black Lives Matter marchers, asked his Secretary of Defense, "Can't you just shoot them? Shoot them in the legs or something?"

And so, it is outrageous to ask how we didn't see Nazism coming when we have somehow accommodated a murderous racism for centuries. Nevertheless, I am asking that. For my own part, I've sorted and sifted and haven't come up with much of an answer for how I missed Andrei's poisonous hatred, except that sometimes I am snow blind, lost in my own whiteness, sometimes I am too trusting, sometimes I'd rather proceed according to my assumptions than check them against what is right in front of me. Whatever constitutes my naïveté is bound up with hope, so that it seems to me now that a true sobriety, a true clarity, can only be had by untangling the two. I can't give up hope — for justice, for peace, for a culture less hospitable to hate — but the failure to grasp how far we are from those things puts those I love in danger. There are days when the news is so old I despair, but there are others when outrage turns to resolve.

> *Andrei, OK, here goes: You and I are enemies. You knew that before I did. We are enemies beyond any possible forgiveness. You're a threat to my family, to my grandchildren, four of them now, and to others I love. There will never be peace between us. You believe the solution to your suffering is to make others suffer, as if you could dilute the poison in your heart by spreading it around. So I do not wish you further harm. But I do not wish you well. It wouldn't surprise me to find out you're dead. I heard your howl from the depths and I understood that you were already dead, if not to me then to yourself. So no, it would not surprise me if you, or someone else, finished the job. I recognize the ghost you are, your abysmal emptiness a cyclone of hate. And if I am being honest, news of your death would come as a relief: one racist Nazi misogynist fewer in the world of my grandchildren. As for your romance with Europe, congratulations! You've found an identity — Shakespeare, as helpful a touchstone of European culture as any, anticipated you in Richard III: "And therefore, since I cannot prove a lover, / To entertain these fair well-spoken days, / I am determined to prove a villain, / And hate the idle pleasures of these days." I should thank you for "waking me the fuck up" to the clear and present danger you and others like you represent. Now I'm resolved to fight. I was going to say "if it comes to that," but it has already come to that; it has always come to that. I see it clearly now. Yes, I should thank you at least for that.*

BACKTALK AND BACKLASH: The Aims, Impact, and Value of Memoir

> "To employ a textual structure which cracks wide open the whole literary convention of an age seems in more than one case to be the only means by which truth and literature can be reconciled."
>
> — Richard Coe, *When the Grass Was Taller*

REMEMBERING, QUESTIONING, AND wondering about the past is an elemental human act. We look for meaning in our experience, and our cultures provide the categories of discourse we use. From binary choices to the complexities of our mother tongue, the making of meaning is thus mediated by precedent and permission. The shaping of memory into a work of literature is an act of faith in the possibility of meaning. I believe that keeping that possibility alive, granting that permission, is the essential work of the memoirist. Mnemosyne, Memory, was, is, and ever shall be mother of all the muses.

It may be that the ascendance of memoir since the 1990's stems from the overload experienced by writers faced with a torrent of propaganda that aims to shape consensus through our pervasive media. In this situation, a growing number of writers have come to feel they can only trust the frail first-person narrator sifting and weighing memories to affirm the existence of a reality beyond the one described so loudly and incessantly not by human beings, but by talking money. Their telling, their honesty and willingness to stand by their words, is a kind of backtalk, a refusal of the lies that a culture derived from profit-seeking uses to numb, subdue, and trap us into a politically de-fanged and spiritually neutered consensus, a Plato's cave of touchscreens, clickbait, instant thrills.

In other words, the rise of memoir that began at the close of "the American century" might best be understood as a corrective to the sheer amount of fictional distortion that has accumulated in a society whose history has been plundered and commodified and staged. Memoirs may be our ongoing "truth and reconciliation hearings," life by life and book by book. It's no wonder that this makes some uncomfortable: after all, there can be no truthful account without an accounting. The poet Lucille Clifton put it succinctly; here in its entirety is her poem, "why some people be mad at me sometimes":

> they ask me to remember
> but they want me to remember
> their memories
> and I keep on remembering
> mine

The desire for amnesty can become a costly amnesia. We tend to most want amnesty when we are exhausted and the hope of justice, of setting things right again, is lost. To the extent that memoirists refuse this comfortable despair, their work can be seen as carrying political, even revolutionary, meaning.

"The struggle of the people against power," wrote Milan Kundera, "is the struggle of memory against forgetting," and those involved in that work are more than narcissists for sale, licking their wounds in public, as threatened power, wielding a sneer, often seeks to portray them. Faced with disinformation, the cynical cultivation of profitable compulsions, history as theme park, and lives increasingly defined by a pop-culture grid and nudged this way and that by algorithms, the memoirist beats a tactical retreat to real, necessarily subjective experience, as a starting point for reclaiming an authentic relation to the world.

Kundera, in exile, called the communist president of Czechoslovakia "The President of Forgetting". Here, in the 1980's, during the dark advent of the great, empty pseudo-culture of consumerism, brought to us through every tinny speaker in every fast-food restaurant ceiling, through mega-plex theatres and cable TV, on the cover of every slick and content-free magazine clogging the shelves, we had an amnesiac actor in the White House. After he left, we were told that for some time he had been suffering from dementia.

It is easier than ever to lie. New media have made it much easier to repeat a lie over and over until it becomes the truth. This has always been a fundamental stratagem of the propagandist, but it used to take a lot longer to lodge untruths in the public mind. Each new untruth is easier to lodge there now because it is congruent with its predecessors, and the most recent bits of disinformation, many iterations now from fact, need not even be plausible. Memoirists, those who are honest, who take their work in the form seriously, are at the very least grit in this machinery manufacturing mass reality. As such, they seem to incite backlash from captious cultural gatekeepers who may or may not be aware of the political dimension of their reactionary disapproval.

For a time, and to an extent still, memoirists have served as handy scapegoats. Never mind that we are being lied to by media, by advertisers, by government, 24/7, 365 days a year. People play along, shrug, take the attitude, "What can you expect?" But let a memoirist misremember the color of the dress she was wearing or the weather on the weekend of the big game, and she is a liar.

A memoir is a representation of the author's encounter with memory. It is a compromise with the demands of narrative and of that medium we call a book. It is less a record of the past than the record of a sustained questioning, a reflective authorial inquiry. Although a memoirist agrees (or certainly should) to respect the facts as they can be known and not to deliberately change them, the memoir is not a photo, it is more a drawing or a painting or a poem, necessarily impressionistic, subjective. In other words, it is art.

In 1996, just after I'd published the memoir *Half the House*, David Samuels, in *Civilization*, the magazine of the Library of Congress, took aim at the increase in first-person nonfiction in an essay tellingly entitled "Mad About Me." After acknowledging the genius of Frank McCourt's *Angela's Ashes*, Samuels began the sophomoric sneering that his title heralds. "Oprah Winfrey and Montel Williams, beware! Stories of alcoholism and recovery, of addiction to sex, of incestuous fathers and other childhood traumas too numerous to mention, have broken free from the talk-show circuit and are arriving by the truckload at a bookstore near you." In the face of such baiting, a memoirist might ask if Samuels would also agree that novels that tell of interlocking painful relationships, betrayals, indecision, infidelities, struggle, have broken free from the daytime soaps and are headed to a bookstore near you? Novels like *Madame Bovary, Anna Karenina, The Wings of the Dove, Absalom, Absalom*. Of course he wouldn't.

Samuels' essay illustrated for me the difficulty one encounters beginning from the wrong assumptions. I do not know what a memoir is. I don't find most definitions very helpful. On the other hand, I don't know what a novel is, either, and still believe that its very name suggests that it will remain a healthy genre only so long as it continues to elude the captivity of a definition. In any case, the difference between the two is certainly not as pat as "fiction lies; autobiography tells the truth," the straw man Samuels goes on to knock down in his essay. Most memoirists are frank in allowing that their works are re-creations, products of what artistry they have been able to bring to bear in searching for a narrative shape. The larger question has to do with the relation between memory and imagination: in a memoir, the imagination serves memory; in fiction, it is most often the other way around, with memory indentured to imagination. Both can be ways of speaking the truth. Both can be ways of lying.

But Samuels was by no means the only dog barking at the caravan. Articles in *The New York Times, Washington Post, Boston Globe*, and elsewhere all seemed to agree that memoir is a third rate genre written by victims licking their unseemly wounds in public. Mostly this turn of the century backlash was driven by the media's unceasing appetite for controversy, for removing complexity and replacing context with contest. For example, I recall an NPR program in which the host interviewed his guests, Frank Conroy and James Salter, by way of a factitious argument that somehow memoirists were a threat to novelists. Of course it didn't come off since Conroy and Salter both hold dual citizenships in the countries of fiction and memoir. In fact, at one point in the program, it appeared the game was over when the interviewer lobbed his serve out of bounds by asking Conroy if the memoir was to blame for the death of the novel. Conroy, clearly taken aback, answered of course that the novel is not dead.

At another point in that program, the host asked his guests about the literary value of unsavory personal details like alcoholism, violence, and perversion. He seemed unaware that one might need to treat those subjects explicitly in order to make sense of the rest of the story, that one can't arrive at anything like the truth by placing certain aspects of one's life, one's story, off-limits. Worse, he seemed unaware that in asking whether such things should be included in a work of literature he had drifted from a discussion of how those subjects might best be treated and was talking instead about what was, in fact, censorship, even if it was couched as bourgeois distaste: *This is why we can't have nice things.*

The aesthete and the reactionary both deny the reality that the private and public spheres are twin arenas where the same ethical and political battles take place. We are all children not only of our families, but of our communities, our country, our culture, our historical moment. This may be a truism, but it is one, it seems, that the present zeitgeist wants us to forget.

When my father, who had grown up in the depression, returned from the butchery to which he was exposed at the age of nineteen, he was told he was one of the good guys, one of those who had saved the world from tyranny. Like so many others, all he wanted in the aftermath of horror was a private life, the illusion of an escape from history.

Those of us who grew up during the postwar years (as opposed to the ahistorical fiction called "the 50's", a time of peace and plenty which did not include the Korean War, McCarthyism, or the constant terrifying threat of atomic attack) were born into some version of a shell-shock ward. It was a tile and chrome world of survivors who heard, with understandable relief and a tragic credulity, the gospel of forgetfulness and were happy to believe it: you must put the past behind you; you mustn't dwell on the past; that was then, this is now. We, their children, had no history, but we lived in the aftermath of war, in the emotional rubble of our parents' rages and sorrow. As we came of age in the era of "the balance of terror," and "Mutually Assured Destruction" and learned what had happened only years before in Europe and Asia, we were enjoined to forget it. The gospel of forgetfulness is alive and well today and in the literary realm it informs much of the clucking and sneering at memoir that continues today.

If we cannot forget the atrocities of recent history, the least we can do is deny we've been affected by them: all those pesky wars, mass murders, inequities, genocides, threats of planetary death. In this project we will be abetted by psychology and self-help texts that treat the individual as either well- or maladapted, and the family as if it existed under a bell jar. What meanings are encouraged, celebrated, sanctioned as truth will be those expressed in comfortably apolitical psychological terms; i.e. it's all in your head.

Memoir's ascendance as a genre is more or less concurrent with the rise of trauma studies and an appreciation of the long lasting, even multigenerational, consequences of atrocity, whether personal or political.

And the backlash to trauma studies was similar to that against memoir in its character (denial) and its virulence (a sneering disdain) during the turn of the century; both comprised what's been called "the memory wars." In both cases an established order, a way of seeing things, was being called into question by unwelcome information. It hardly bears going into here, but it's worth pointing to Jeffrey Moussaieff Masson's *The Assault on Truth* as a book that incited ferocious resistance. In it, he unveils the fact that Freud himself caved to the professional backlash he met when he bore witness to the suffering and symptoms of his patients. Masson met a backlash of his own in the person of journalist Janet Malcolm who attacked him in the pages of *The New York Review of Books* and later in her book *In the Freud Archives.*

Suffice to say a great deal has been written and fought over about memory ever since, and those who were writing memoir found themselves in the thick of the battle. Today, however, now that certain undeniable truths have surfaced — about the Catholic Church, the Boy Scouts, the Magdalen laundries, the Indian schools, and on and on — we can see clearly that most of what was called *repressed memory* on the part of survivors of violence, especially childhood sexual violence was, in fact, memory *suppressed* by institutional power and control. This suppression of the truth not only creates gaps in the record, it discourages truth telling. The drama of Dr. Christine Blasey Ford's testimony at the confirmation hearing for justice Brett Kavanaugh offers a case in point: the futility of the truth in the face of patriarchal power's tantrums abets a silence that radiates across the country from its truthless capital, dissolving most questions of accountability in the digestive juices of "Why bother?"

Historical silences, whatever unspeakable trauma has engendered them, are referred to by trauma therapists as "present absences." The presence of a signifier without a referent, the presence of an absence of story, of memory, in the individual psyche and in the historical record (with its obvious impact on our culture, now almost completely given over to entertaining distractions) creates certain dead zones in consciousness and redactions in the historical record that require various detours and work-arounds. Perhaps the most important discovery of trauma researchers is that these silences, placeholders for things unspeakable, persist across generations, even after their subject is forgotten, and that these psychic voids are heritable, epigenetically, filially, culturally.

Psychoanalyst Galit Atlas, in her book *Emotional Inheritance*, writes about her client Noah, who had "an incessant preoccupation with death." Later, she discovered that he was named after a brother who had died at eight months old, just before Noah was born. His parents never told him because they felt he should not have to carry that weight. Obviously, he carried it anyway — and without the means — the requisite understanding — to come to terms with it. This is what's meant by "the presence of the absence." Elizabeth Rosner, in her book, *Survivor Café*, which considers the many and varied ways that trauma is passed down through generations, points us to a phrase in Spanish, "la teta asustada" that refers to inherited grief — literally, the teat of sorrow, the breast of sadness, the milk of grief.

There is a role for forgetting, of course, but suppression of memory and hiding the truth is not forgetting. And there is a *time* for forgetting as well, and it is always *after* an event has been understood and integrated into a narrative (personal, familial, or societal;) i.e. after it has ceased to have unwanted consequences.

In a country founded on the largest act of genocide in history, a country built by kidnapping people from their homes and trafficking them as commodities, as labor and as wombs for future labor, as "resources," we are so far from the truth, so habitually deflective, inattentive, and ahistorical that it's as if a gag once placed over an ancestor's mouth has become a ubiquitous fashion accessory and much of what is celebrated in our art and literature is the elegance of the latest gag's design. In any case, the aggregate of these many silences, things deemed unspeakable, is a great weight on successive generations.

America is not of course alone in the manufacture of silence, but America is my country, one where it seems privacy is only valued when it is protecting the secret transgressions of the powerful.

The memoirs I cherish are those that work to name those silences, that defy the injunction to go along to get along, that enact that search for the truth that is the closest thing we have to the truth. Meaning derives from that pursuit, a search driven by the increasingly desperate need for a course correction.

I believe that by now I have heard all the arguments against memoir, including the unreliability of memory, the many distortions involved in constructing a narrative, and the necessarily biased view of even the most credible storyteller. There is even an argument that holds that experience itself is, of course, chaos, and that as soon as you attach language to it you have falsified it. In this view, everything is fiction as soon as it turns into language. But that's like saying that the air we breathe is changed in our lungs — of course it is, and that change, that exchange, keeps us alive. The same goes for storytelling, the primary way that human beings make meaning, noting consequences, chains of events, patterns we call true. Story sustains us. It is the way we integrate experience and claim it as our own. Finally, it is not a question of whether some objective truth can be known, since even in the world of particle physics, we now know that the observer is always part of the event. Or, as the poet Terrance Hayes has written,

> *Not even two eyes in the same head see the same things.*
>
> "Self-Portrait As the Mind of a Camera"

it is a question of honesty; not a matter of truth but of truthfulness.

We have a strange idea that the truth is simple, that it is something you blurt out. No artist or scientist would ever agree with that formulation! The truth is always something you arrive at after painstaking investigation, and the truth of our own lives is no exception. The memoir is governed by a radical honesty that accepts the facts as they are known and as they may be further discovered in the process of remembering, researching, and writing. Writing doesn't come from knowing. Knowing comes from writing. Writing comes from unknowing.

The aesthete's nearly theological idea of art for art's sake depends at least in part on writing for posterity, but it's hard to sell the concept of posterity to those raised in the shadow of Hiroshima, and the twin state-terrorisms of the Cold War, not to mention the generations following, faced with ecological catastrophe. Those who know we have been and are still only half a step from a real, not mythic Armageddon, aren't buying it. Memoirists ask, in the aftermath of upheaval — and what has the last century been but a series of upheavals, disruptions, breakages? — how could this have happened? And by extension, how does this keep on happening?

Some years ago, frustrated by the ahistorical education my graduate students had received, I developed a course called "The Twentieth Century in the First Person: Memoir as the Literature of Witness." The students were bright and ambitious, verbal virtuosos; one of them asked me if it was true that Stalin was a communist.

The course was predicated on the idea that writers are, beyond all else, witnesses to their time, and that memoirists can often provide a more palpable sense of the impact and consequence of events than a historian's necessarily academic perspective. Memoirs can offer the felt experience of the past, the view from below, as it were, not only the dates and stats and documents, not only the facts, but also the hopes, fears, beliefs, regrets, and desires that animate the facts. If my students were to become the poets, the novelists, the essayists and memoirists of the future (and many of them have) I wanted them to be able to situate themselves in relation to the past, to the ways it informs the present and requires us to bear witness to the ongoing challenges that have come tumbling down to us from upstream.

Beginning with Robert Graves' serio-comic recollections of trench warfare in WWI in *Goodbye to All That,* we moved through Nadezdha Mandelstam's *Hope Against Hope*; Primo Levi's *Survival in Auschwitz*; Zhu Xiao Di's *30 Years in a Red House* about his childhood during Mao's Cultural Revolution. We read, back to back, Mark Mathabane's *Kaffir Boy* about his childhood under apartheid and Alexandra Fuller's memoir of her Afrikaans family *Don't Let's Go to the Dogs Tonight*. We moved chronologically toward the near past, asking how these writers had wrested significance from their experience of their times, and looking for ways to adapt their methods to finding the shape of our own narratives.

Three memoirs were student favorites year after year, and all three are accounts not of their authors' first-hand experience, but of their quest to understand the world they'd been bequeathed, the legacies of their parents and grandparents. Peter Balakian, in *Black Dog of Fate*, only wants to understand the eccentricities of his beloved grandmother, but as he proceeds, hand over hand, question after question, he uncovers the truth of the impact of events half a world and half a century away: the Armenian Genocide (which has remained his major focus in a long and celebrated career.) In her remarkable *Good Neighbors, Bad Times*, Mimi Schwartz, author also of *When History Is Personal* (which eloquently speaks to my point here) returns to her father's village in Germany to try to verify his tales of righteous Christians who hid their Jewish townsmen from the Nazis. And *After Long Silence*, in which Helen Fremont, after discovering her own Jewish identity, hidden from her by her parents, reassembles the truth of her parents' wartime story, and in the process is restored to the truth of her identity, even to the extent of being reunited with family who survived the Shoah.

In all three of these works, the search for the truth is the story. In all three it is artfully told, and in all three the bespoke form of the book is itself the arrival, after great investigative effort, of meaning. To tell a story from your life, invulnerable to discovery, is to turn life into ink; to contend with the questions the writing raises, by research, soul-searching, and considering the accounts of others, and find the formal grace that makes it all a story is to turn life into art.

"True stories have no end," Charles Fish tells us in his masterful 1995 memoir, *In Good Hands: the Keeping of a Family Farm*, "but a storyteller must find boundaries, or else from three small sentences in a diary he could be drawn to the beginning of the world."

The beginning of the world. In his essay, "My Caedmon: Thinking about Poetic Vocation," Allen Grossman reminds us that the first poet in English, called upon by his fellows to sing a song, something familiar, as they sat before the fireplace, declined, having no song to sing. Later, "Caedmon was commanded by someone in a dream to sing something. Confessing himself unable to think what or how to sing, he was directed to sing, in his dream, the beginning of the creatures. And he did so. Upon awaking, in the presence of persons of authority in the monastery (Whitby) where he worked, Caedmon remade, again on demand, his poetic text."

Memoirists, regarded for the time being as poets (and many of them are), can be viewed as singers who found no other song to sing and sang the beginning of the world, this world; i.e. how this world became the particular shape of this consciousness. Mary Karr, Mark Doty, Tracy K. Smith, David Mura, Natasha Trethewey, Gregory Orr, R. Dwayne Betts — all have written exquisitely about becoming known to themselves, about the ways the past and present conjugate to become the future.

If it is true that history cannot be understood without psychology, nor an individual's psychology be understood without situating that person in history (and clearly I believe so) then the coming-of-age story, the kind of memoir the critic Richard Coe calls "The Childhood," is also a kind of backtalk. One of the chief ways we are uprooted from our histories is the creation of a generic, sentimentalized idea of childhood, and the best memoirs disallow such a caricature. Children are cute, there's no arguing with that, but none of us ever thought of *ourselves* as cute, especially back when we were suffering the daily puzzlements and injustices of childhood. In reality, as children we contend, for the first time, with the superstructure of adult untruth; we encounter the world without explanations, expectations, and excuses. But we also experience moments of respite from all of that when we know, wordlessly, who we are, what we are, what it all means, although it can take a lifetime to even begin to articulate that understanding. Childhood is a time of grave confusion and painful realizations — "It's not fair!" Our emotions are volatile and fierce. All too often it is the site of atrocity and abiding suffering. And yet, it is also the temple of the sublime.

Sometimes I think that because it is so difficult to reconcile the wonder and horror of childhood, people make a choice to remember only one or the other. It is very nearly impossible to write a whole book that one-dimensional, at least not one that anyone would want to read. Thinking of my own boyhood: when it wasn't horrible it was wonderful; when it wasn't wonderful, it was horrible. Sometimes, but not often, it was neither wonderful nor horrible, and, particularly as I got older, there were times when although it was horrible it was also wonderful, or when it was wonderful and at the same time horrible.

To balance or offset corruption, violence, ignorance, I was given the smell of greenhouse soil, the wonder of staring fish, the laughter of grownups, the songs of my mother, the cool shade under a wooden bridge, the smell of a baseball mitt, the feel of a nightcrawler as you tug it from the wet ground, the trellises loaded down to crooked near-collapse by roses, the wedding cake rosettes of colored paint on a house-painter's spattered shoes. It was enough.

Would I go through such a childhood again? The question is academic. I have. I will. Again and again. And everything I am, it goes without saying, has grown from that time before time, that brief time when time was giving and not yet taking. Time and again I am moved by the flash of sunlight on rippling water and the cold fire of reflections licking the trunks of a riverbank's trees. I am what I have kept of time's presents. I don't recall ever choosing what to keep. Perhaps I am what's chosen me.

Writing a memoir becomes, eventually, like turning over a circuit board and seeing how the connections have been made. Going down below street-level. Checking on the worn-out, maybe dangerous plumbing and wiring, learning how things really work. And finding that little has been "built to code." This is more than recalling events and stringing them like beads. This is a do or die existential command from deep in a dream. Those who merely "play the market" with a "hot" story are impostors, pretenders, and worse. The memories that animate the memoirist are not the same ones as those that animate the raconteur. Memoirists are driven by perplexity, by shock at their own ignorance of how time has unspooled and become history. The acronym WTF? about sums it up.

I don't believe most people know how to read this genre. Popular culture seems to recognize curiosity and entertainment as the only two possible motives for reading about another's experience. Indeed, these are the memoirs publishers seek, the ones that sell. All books in our consumer culture exist within this strange tension: is a book a commodity or a mode of discourse?

In any case, to set out to appeal — one might as well say pander — to readers' expectations seems to me to forfeit the potential insight and understanding that await writers who conduct a deep and honest inquiry, which includes an appreciation of the fallibility of memory and an understanding that putting experience into words, particularly written words, is a kind of translation. Memoirists and their readers should never forget that a memoir is a complex representation — a re-presentation — of remembering; an exercise in subjectivity, in honesty, in art.

I realize I am staking out the high ground here. So be it. There is power verging on prophecy in the genre. Honest memoirists discover their destiny: not their destiny hereafter, not some soothsayer's fortune, but what causes and effects, influences and resistances, circumstances and compulsions have been, mostly unnoticed, at work in their lives. They discover what subjects, predicates, objects, and modifiers have sentenced them. They come to understand what the future was.

Maybe this engenders a similar process in readers. Some of these readers are also writers. Maybe that's enough to explain the popularity of memoir. But I suspect the current runs much deeper than that.

According to Plotinus, who enriched and humanized the Rome of his day by re-membering the body of Hellenic knowledge that had been sundered, or dis-membered, by imperialism and war, "Memory is for those who have forgotten."

Now, you can read that sentence to mean, merely, that you have no need to remember unless you have first forgotten, a reading that seems both obvious and true. It seems so because this is the way we usually understand memory; i.e., that faculty which allows us to recapture something that we once had, or at least almost had, before it slipped into unavailability like a dropped pop-up, or a fish hooked tenuously and lost, or a scene glimpsed from the window of a moving train.

But I understand that statement a bit differently. I choose to think of this neo-Platonist's shimmering, ambiguous remark as a description of the artist's vocation, one that grounds that calling in social responsibility, in justice; one that believes in the power of the art it produces. In other words, Memory is for *the sake of* those who have forgotten. For the love of, for the health of, for the sustenance of those who have forgotten.

This way of looking at Plotinus' statement also bears in mind the fact that Mnemosyne, or Memory, is the mother of all the muses. Hers is the power of continuity that, shaped by the arts, brings forth from the past not monsters but recognizable, unique variations of her pattern. For those who have forgotten.

Ultimately, the commingling of past and present includes the dead as well as the living, our forbears as well as our children. The memoirist's disciplined practice includes an openness to grief, regret, and remorse in order to see reality clearly. This extrication from lies, shame, and silence, this liberation, is the result of many individual acts of truth-telling performed by choosing this word or phrase over that, by honoring the integrity of each event as opposed to modifying its contours to fit, by the quest to understand how time, along with place, race, class, and culture, has unfolded character and determined history.

Anamnesis, the remembering of the dismembered past, is a sustained stance toward the world, a political commitment as well as a literary and spiritual undertaking. As Elie Weisel has said, "Memory is not only a victory over time, it is a triumph over injustice." If forgetfulness, amnesia, is a kind of death, then the kind of restoration and reintegration of experience or history is not only life-affirming for the practitioner, but also confers, in the hands of a skillful artist, a kind of new life on those who would have otherwise disappeared.

Sometime during the years I was at work on the memoir *Half the House*, a friend asked me if writing it was healing for me. *Oh, brother*, I thought. Here we go again. I found it exasperating that people continually made the assumption that one writes memoir for chiefly therapeutic reasons.

But I hid my frustration so as not to give offense; the question had been asked in good faith. I offered an answer designed to allow her to reinterpret the pained look on my face as a search for the right word. "I would say... that... that it's helping me." She looked a little bit stung, no doubt picking up on my reaction. So I continued. "It helps me integrate some themes that persist in my life. So I guess, in that sense, I'd have to say yes. Yes, it *is* healing for me." She smiled, searched my eyes, and nodded. I felt like an ass. Why had I behaved so defensively?

My friend didn't realize the challenge her question represented. I am glad she asked it though, because it allowed me to see that my bristly attitude was largely a reaction to the way the literary world had used that word "healing" to dismiss the genre. I had been trapped in a cartoonish definition of healing; and I had been imagining and feeling the sneer of a composite ghost, part English Department, part *New York Times Book Review*, part *The Paris Review*. As is often the case, it was an encounter with an actual reader, and not with the phantom of high modernism, that meager inheritance, that tipped me into a real answer.

In fact, to write memoir is to reenact the process of becoming, to tap into that dynamic dimension of yourself, to try not only to describe past experience, but to feel it again and understand that feeling as power, your own continuing power, in the present. Besides, if people feel the need to heal from their childhoods, doesn't that raise serious questions about our social and political life?

When I teach writing, as I have now for decades, I encourage my students to make a list of the questions that keep them up at night. Now this is really asking for it, in every sense of that phrase. It is an invitation to them and a great responsibility for their teacher. I encourage them to find the question that continues to engender further questions, and then, as they proceed, I urge them to keep writing these further questions in the margins, to be taken up later. I quote Vivian Gornick's remark to the effect that the quality of first person nonfiction is measured by the depth of its inquiry.

Among my students have been: a young Bosnian woman who narrowly, miraculously, escaped the Serb militia who killed her parents and several of her neighbors at a roadside checkpoint; and a young woman writing about her researches into the underworld murders of her parents in a motel when she was three; a young man just home from combat in Afghanistan; a young woman who stepped out for groceries and returned to find her sister dead on the kitchen floor, her throat cut. Countless stories of abuse, eating disorders, rapes, hospitalizations, overdoses.

At night I'd lay awake thinking of my student, then nine years old, lying beneath her parents' bodies in a pit until she heard the soldiers' drunken laughter stop and the trucks depart. Or of any number of the workshop manuscripts on my desk. These were bright, beautiful young people trying to tell the truth in their writing, trying to come to terms with their experience, their suffering. What's more, I teach graduate courses in a college of the arts, and these were serious young artists committed to fashioning something beautiful and important from that pain.

Discussions with colleagues about the pedagogy of teaching nonfiction writing would invariably lead to someone blurting out, "I'm not a therapist!" I said it myself, used it as a flimsy protection, a pretext for not engaging too deeply with my students' suffering.

And yet, it depends what you mean by that term. There is certainly an opportunity, as well as the means --- if we believe what we say about the power of the written word — to reconstitute, to reintegrate lives shattered by the last quarter century or so, which happens to have been their one and only youth. It seems to me the responsibility of adults to embrace that opportunity.

I have my own history of trauma and I had been leaning hard on that experience to fashion my responses to students' efforts, not to mention orchestrating a workshop, trying to keep it safe for everyone. I was exhausted. And so, I spoke with a friend who is a therapist, asking for a referral; not for my students, for me.

He asked me what kind of support I had for the work I was doing. He asked me point blank, "Who's got your back?" and went on to explain that people in clinical practice always have supervision, preferably group supervision, where they can discuss difficult cases and rely on the advice and support of other practitioners. "Yes, but," I said, "I'm not in clinical practice." And I said it: "I am not a therapist." I raised other objections. I was not trying to fix my students. "Good,"" he said, "because you can't. I don't try to fix my patients either."

"I'm trying to teach them to make art."

"In other words," he said, "to make something coherent of what's happened to them?"

We talked about the probable origin of the word "therapist." I suspect he knew that as a writer, a poet, this etymological approach would really get me. In the ancient Asklepian tradition, he said, somewhat older but largely concurrent with the Hippocratic tradition of healing, the distressed came to the temple to heal themselves by performing certain rites. During their time in the temple, they were surrounded by statuary and paintings; plays were performed, stories were told, poetry recited. They remained there until the night they had the dream that would heal them of their malaise, their disempowerment. Then they painted, or wrote a play or a story or a poem to leave behind them at the temple. According to my therapist friend, those who attended them, who helped in the creation of the work they would leave behind, work which would become a part of the temple's rites going forward, were called the *therapeutiae.*

Stories that are read and loved and kept as our own can begin as extremely personal explorations, containing the kind of knowledge and experience that until now would have been censored by government, or publishers, or, via shame, by the authors themselves (indeed preventing many from authoring their "lives" at all, the internal censor is so strong.)

The backtalk I've been writing about here is born from indignation at corruption, dishonesty, vulgarity; at a world in which consumer capitalism has undermined the idea of personhood more completely and tragically than any collectivist ideology has ever managed to do. I'm writing in defense of the genre, but mainly against a simplistic definition of it, whether by scornful critics, hungry publishers, naive readers, or those writers who are always telling me they have a great story and that one day they will "write it down."

I believe that the story you know is either the story you've been told, or the one you've been telling yourself. That's fine, but the only reason to spend years spinning a story from your own guts is that the story you've held onto no longer suffices. The process of writing a memoir is an attempt at discovery: how did I get to be the person who finds myself needing to write this story? What forces have been at work, unseen, since before I was born? How do I inhabit history? How does history inhabit and shape me? Inhibit or propel me? It's not about telling your reader what happened or teaching your reader anything you think you know; it's about making an inquiry into the mystery of your life that goes deep enough to be about the reader's life as well.

That's the ultimate purpose of memoir: to illumine the life of the reader, and perhaps to inspire the kind of inquiry that leads to a personal emancipation from shame and silence and the layers of untruth — lies, false assumptions, outworn tropes — under which we've all been buried. As such, writing memoir, and reading it, can have a profoundly healing power, a revolutionary power that takes place one book, one reader — one mind, one heart — at a time.

TO HELL AND BACK: After Long Silence by Helen Fremont

I NO LONGER REMEMBER the first time I read *After Long Silence.* I have been pressing it on my friends, colleagues, and students ever since it first appeared. When people complain that memoir is a narcissist's genre, that its truths are not only specious but small, I tell them to read it. When people claim there is nothing new to say about the Holocaust, I tell them to read it. When students sign up for my graduate seminar in the memoir, it is there on the syllabus as an example of all that the genre can accomplish in the service of memory and history.

After Long Silence is among a handful of memoirs that successfully reckon with the consequences of the twentieth century's atrocities and dislocations; that it does so in a manner by turns lyrical, elegiac, ferocious, playful, and dramatic makes it an extraordinary piece of literary art. Above and beyond its moving story and vivid characters, it earns its understandings, counts the cost of untruths, even those required to survive, and asks hard questions about love, loyalty, family, and identity.

Raised in the Midwest as a Catholic, the author discovers in her mid-30s that in fact she is not who she has been told she is, that she and her sister Lara have been inhabiting, with diminishing success, a fiction her parents created and maintained, and that in fact she is the daughter of Polish Jews whose families perished in the Holocaust. Out of the deepest psychic necessity, the two sisters begin a quest to discover what happened to their parents, to restore their families, and to forge from the truth identities more congruent with the history of their family and people.

What Fremont discovers, that her mother is among the few survivors of the massacre of Jews in her home town, that her father survived six years in the Russian gulag, is the result of a perseverance she clearly inherited. Her unearthing of the bones of the story, however, also threatens her mother's fragile truce with the past and wakens ghosts that make a happy ending impossible.

From the memoir's first pages we are given to understand that the triangle of mother-father-child here is not merely a Freudian schema placed under a literary bell jar for study. This family's life, not to say its fate, is shaped not by drives and complexes and discontents, but by the charnel houses of Nazism, the brutalities of Italian Fascism, and the frozen killing fields of Stalinism.

In answer to five-year-old Helen's curiosity, her parents concur: her grandparents, all of them, died "in a bomb." Period.

> Childhood was a strange place to find oneself after so much history.
>
> As the baby of the family, I was the tail end of that history, and by the time I would try to make sense of it, it had been erased by my elders.

Fremont's parents, especially her mother, claim good reasons for their decision to leave their European Jewish past behind:

> When I was small, maybe five or six, my mother came to my bed every night to tuck me in. She would teach me the sign of the cross in six languages: Polish, Russian, German, Italian, French, and English. Each night I selected a language, and we said the sign of the cross in that language: In the name of the Father, the Son, and the Holy Spirit, Amen. Then she taught me the prayer Our Father in those languages, and I rehearsed them until I knew them by heart. I loved the way the gumdrop syllables rolled off the tongue in Italian and the way the consonants crashed in German; I loved the tongue-twisting sounds of Polish and the fur-lined purr of French and Russian. And of course, I loved our conspiracy — my mother's and mine. It was our time alone, our time together, and she was sending me into a night of sleep, protected by a God who could respond to me in any language, under any sky.
>
> What I didn't understand was that my mother was equipping me with the means of survival: proof of my Catholicism to anyone in a dozen countries.

The trouble, of course, is that a history filled with omissions and ellipses is not only a fiction, but a continually renewed false identity that robs us of authenticity in the present and subtly poisons everything. At the same time, who could blame a woman who had traversed wartime Europe, the daughter of orthodox Jews, passing her self off as a Polish Catholic, an Italian (male) soldier, and Maria, sister-in-law of an Italian count, over and over "acting for her life," for believing in the magical power of fiction to transform reality?

It is nearly a perfect inversion: just as her mother and her aunt Zosia (another deeply complex figure deftly drawn) relied on fiction for their survival, Fremont and her sister must turn the sleeve right-side-out, so to speak, and uncover the life-giving truth of their identities. Their sleuthing drives the larger narrative and provides the structure for the book, and although it lays bare and exacerbates the stresses of the family, its momentum is that of history righting itself, a kind of moral force that has its own power:

> We were on fire; all our talk and theories went out the window. In the end, a burning house follows only the laws of physics. We were consumed by our need to know.

And yet the truth of the past, the sensible human truth beyond the names and dates, cannot be arrived at except by an act of the imagination, by supposing, by fiction's magical power. In this respect *After Long Silence* is the perfect example of the memoirist's proper use of the imagination — as a faculty, subordinate to memory and research, in the service of unearthing and revivifying the truth. Adherence to the known facts as they are found in records and testimony does not make the past less imaginary. To paraphrase Gertrude Stein: there is no back then back there. As Fremont writes of her deeper inquiry:

> Stories always change for a reason. The truth lies somewhere between the reasons and the stories.

Another way to think about this, and a more useful way than the usual smackdown between memoir as truth and fiction as made-up stuff, is to acknowledge what cognitive science tells us: that memory and imagination are closely related faculties. It is not a question of one or the other of this pair, it is a question of which partner is leading the dance.

In Fremont's skilled hands, literary imagination becomes a precision instrument, a tool of empathy, and the adult fulfillment of a promise made to her mother as a child:

> "When I grow up," I told my parents when I was eight years old, "I'm going to write the story of your lives." My mother smiled. At the time I knew almost nothing of their lives — the past was a mystery, part romance, part war.

As an example of Fremont's masterful handling of scene, consider this brief but emblematic instance:

> One day, early in the German occupation, my mother told me, Zosia was walking along Krakowska Street with a friend of hers, a young man she knew in high school. A German soldier approached them, smoking a cigarette, his face bathed in July sunshine. Instinctively, Zosia stepped off the sidewalk into the street and continued walking, never raising her eyes. Her friend was not so quick to defer, and the bullet ripped through his forehead. He fell at Zosia's feet, eyebrows raised, his face a map of blood. Zosia kept walking, her feet obeying an unspoken order. Her eyes remained fixed on the cobblestones in front of her. She passed the German without looking up. The faint smell of his cigarette, familiar, acrid. He replaced the revolver in his belt, and his boots receded down the sidewalk behind her. Neither Zosia nor the soldier had broken their gait; between them, Zosia's friend lay at the moment of his mistake, his face flowing into the stones of the street that he should have stepped down to.

Nearly every scene in the book has this quality of being at once itself and standing as emblem for the larger story, each situation a microcosm, each act of survival a kind of precedent for life in the aftermath of the war.

What remains to be said is that the luminosity and sonority of the language in *After Long Silence* is testament to the fact that poetry occurs in prose as well as in verse. This prose is exquisitely modulated, resonant, and supple: somehow there's a whole orchestra in there. (If the human voice has registers Fremont doesn't employ in her prose I'm not aware of them.) And yet this makes perfect sense; this is a book that traces the oldest of poetic journeys — to hell and back — and if you hope to break the heart of Hades, if you make the journey down, if you walk the underworld seeking answers, you had better be singing.

WHATS LOVE GOT TO DO WITH IT?

> Far in the woods they sang their unreal songs,
> Secure. It was difficult to sing in face
> Of the object. The singers had to avert themselves
> Or else avert the object.
>
> — Wallace Stevens, "Credences of Summer"

PAULA VOGEL'S PULITZER prize-winning drama *How I Learned to Drive* is a masterful depiction of the relentless wiles of a single-minded child molester, an acknowledgment of the devastating impact of his assaults on a young girl, and an exploration of the role of alcoholism and gender stereotypes in the sexual abuse of children. It is also, ultimately, a betrayal of children, an affront to adults who have survived such abuse, and a dispiriting moral shrug.

The play, which Vogel has described as her "homage to Lolita," is constructed in reverse chronology, as a series of flashbacks ending with a couplet of scenes that connect the 34 -year-old protagonist, named L'il Bit, with the beginning of her painful alienation 23 years earlier when her Uncle Peck first laid his hands on her budding breasts. "...that day was the last day I lived in my body," L'il Bit tells us. "I've retreated above the neck, and I've lived inside the fire in my head ever since." What Peck gives her, which replaces her body, is her love of the highway, of speed, and he haunts her after his death, grinning at her from the rearview mirror as she drives faster and faster, trying to feel alive.

When I saw the play in a matinee performance at Trinity Rep in Providence, I was prepared to be uncomfortable, not only because as one who was sexually violated as a boy I knew I would find the content disturbing, but also because I'd read reviews that praised the play as a "love story" between a girl and her uncle. However, as Vogel traced, layer by retrospective layer, Li'l Bit's adult dissociation, joylessness, and alcoholism to the relentless pressure of her uncle's advances throughout her girlhood, I found myself completely won over. "Yes, this is how it happens," I said with each manipulation, each carefully constructed double-bind. The 70's term for such paralyzing sorcery, "mindfuck," occurred to me for the first time in a long while. It seemed an apt description of Peck's designs. When finally, as a young woman who has just drunk herself out of college, Li'l Bit gathers the courage to spurn him, I felt satisfied that the critics had got it all wrong.

Then, in a scene that still seems to me tellingly extraneous, L'il Bit suddenly announces that she's forgiven Uncle Peck and that, appreciative of all he has given her, she hopes that his spirit, which she imagines roaming the highways in his car, will find one young girl who can give herself to him entirely as she could not. Saying that she always wanted to ask him one question, she cries out to the heavens, "Who did it to you, Uncle Peck? Were you eleven when he did it to you?"

I was thunderstruck. As I said to a friend, outside in the merciful clarity of a June afternoon, I felt like I'd been sucker-punched.

Putting aside for the moment complex questions of literary ethics, including the question of who has the right to tell the story (Kipling or R.K. Narayan? Zane Gray or Sherman Alexie? Frederick Douglass or Harriet Beecher Stowe?) I have to ask what Vogel thought such a conclusion would accomplish. The play seems to come apart there as surely as if Hamlet had dropped his sword and decided that, after all, his uncle wasn't such a bad guy; or Oedipus, choosing to keep his eyes lodged firmly in their sockets, cried out, "Why can't we all just get along?"

It is hard to know what could be more hurtful and offensive than this demoralizing dramaturgical and ethical collapse; that is, until one reads Vogel's interview in the bulletin of the American Repertory Theater. "My play dramatizes the gifts we receive from the people who hurt us," she insists. Elsewhere, in a television interview, she said the play, "is a love story, a story of healing and forgiving, and about moving on."

It's as if Vogel cannot properly add up the column of figures she's set down. Let's see: scheming to ensnare a child with guilt; playing on a child's fear of abandonment; rubbing a pubescent girl's breasts; plying an adolescent with alcohol; shaming another child, a young boy, into a secret liaison; photographing a child in erotic poses; all these things add up to — forgiveness?

And yet, Vogel's miscalculation is telling and perhaps instructive about the faulty conceptual structure that keeps us from coming to terms with sexual child abuse. In order to arrive at "healing and forgiving," the playwright resorts to a *Deus ex machina*, provided by L'il Bit's breakthrough insight: that Peck must also have been abused as a child! This pernicious bit of psychobabble, the falsehood that men who were themselves abused as children are somehow thus fated through no fault of their own to violate children, becomes within the theatre what it is in the larger culture: the *machina* of disempowerment, the blunting of outrage, the intellectualization of evil, the failure to protect children.

Leaving aside for the moment how personally offensive it is to me as a man sexually violated as a child, it is worth taking the trouble here to examine where this toxic factoid comes from. The U.S. Dept. of Justice claims that 55% of men incarcerated for sexual offenses against children were themselves victimized in boyhood. This means two things. First of all, it means that 45%, nearly half, of child molesters in the prison system were *not* themselves violated as children. Secondly, the sample consists only of those who are convicted perpetrators, not the exponentially larger universe of those who have been victims. One other bit of arithmetic is in order here, since most people remain unaware of it: it is not uncommon for a single pedophile to have hundreds of victims over a period of decades. (I take Peck's preying upon the young boy, Bobby, in Vogel's play as evidence of her understanding of the omnivorous nature of his appetites.) Anyway, let's add it up — let's add up the pain, the self-hatred, the lost childhoods, the mental illness, the alcoholism, the suicides. What do you get? Forgiveness?

Does anyone remember in our New Age, no-fault moral universe, that to forgive is a transitive verb? That forgiveness is a transaction? That it involves penitence, not pity? Not to mention "the firm purpose of amendment?" What is forgiveness if no one has acknowledged wrongdoing, nor asked for it, nor changed their conduct? What is forgiveness in the case of a serial offender preying upon the helpless? What if turning the other cheek is, in fact, offering up the next child?

Much has been made of the fact that Vogel did not make Peck a one-dimensional villain in a trenchcoat. Uncle Peck is not a cartoon monster but a charming man with, "a fire in his heart." (Never mind that, absent the lyricism, that boils down to garden variety alcoholism, hardly an excuse for the ongoing violation of Li'l Bit and the serial molestation of other children.) We never believe that Peck is less than human. His smile is infectious, his wit sharp, his manner gentle; in fact, as with Humbert Humbert, it is his charm and our own response to it that is so chilling. But it remains so only because we are aware, at one and the same time, of the massively evil plundering of a young girl's sense of herself. That he is a predator and not merely a libidinous uncle with lousy boundaries is borne out by the scene in which he lures a young boy by shaming him, promising him he won't tell that he's seen him crying, and offering to exchange secrets with him. Yet we're supposed to believe that Uncle Peck loves L'il Bit because he tells himself he does?

Excuse me for a moment but here I have to tell you a story. A true one, rooted in fact, not psychobabble tricked out as art. When my memoir, *Half the House*, was published, the coach portrayed in the book (and named therein after much wrangling with the publisher's lawyers) was found to be still coaching boys in my hometown. That's not all he was still doing, either. Within a short time this serial rapist of prepubescent boys, Tom Feifel, was under arrest, and the District Attorney's office had nearly two dozen boys who were willing to testify against him. When the story went out on the AP wire, the police began receiving calls, from all over the country, from men in their forties, thirties, twenties, and of course from the parents of young boys who had recently been violated by Feifel. The numbers climbed. "We're at the tip of the iceberg with this," said Gerry Procanyn, the detective who arrested Feifel. "Those who have seen articles or who have purchased the book are calling to let us know that this is not something that happened just six months ago, that they were victims years ago. We've had calls from as far away as Florida."

Procanyn had been involved with both of Feifel's previous arrests. The first took place in 1967, the year I graduated from high school. The charge was sodomy. The mother of the boy Feifel raped, however, chose not to put her child through the further trauma of a trial. The charge was reduced to disorderly conduct.

In 1984, Feifel went before a judge again, this time on charges of "involuntary deviant sexual intercourse and corruption of a minor." He pleaded guilty to the lesser charge in return for a sentence of eighteen months' probation. He also agreed to seek counseling for his "problem."

The District Attorney selected three boys whom she felt were strong enough witnesses. I was there for the trial. Before his sentencing, Feifel told the court — and here's my point — that he loved the boys, and as evidence he protested that he had bought one of them a bicycle.

Not long ago, in my hometown of Cambridge, ten-year-old Jeffrey Curley was promised a bicycle by two neighborhood men whom he believed were his friends. He never got it. He got a 50 gallon Rubbermaid container, though, in which to hide his raped and broken body at the bottom of a New Hampshire river.

"My play dramatizes the gifts we receive from the people who hurt us," Vogel says, as if no one else might have taught L'il Bit how to drive, as if the counterfeit joys of excitement, speed, and alcohol were somehow worth her flunking out of college, her inability to form meaningful relationships, and the loss of her sense of herself as a viable person. I believe that Blake, not subject to our zeitgeist of shrugs, smirks, sneers, and evasions, had it more nearly right when he wrote, "And if blight kill not a tree but it still bear fruit; let none say that the fruit was in consequence of the blight."

Sexual predators require a prodigious level of rationalization to persist in their crimes. But simply because they cannot distinguish between love and hate does not mean that we, who require less denial and fewer untruths to get on with our lives, are similarly incapacitated. I have argued elsewhere that we try to bring our language regarding the sexual abuse of children more in alignment with reality, beginning with the word *pedophile*. The word comes from Greek and means, literally, "one who loves children." What an Orwellian inversion. In place of the term pedophile, let me offer an alternative: pedoscele, from the Latin scelus, meaning "evil deed." Try it. Pedoscele: one who does evil to children.

Pedosceles of course prefer the term pedophile. They believe they are being persecuted for the exercise of their sexuality. They further believe that one day society will emerge from this dark age into an enlightenment that will see them, in retrospect, as an unfairly persecuted group. Where of course these children are to come from remains to be worked out since, when the great day of liberation comes, it is doubtful whether tiny Thailand, so far doing yeoman's duty as a supplier, will be able to meet the increased demand.

"There are two forgivenesses in the play," Vogel tells us in the A.R.T. interview. "One forgiveness for Peck, but the most crucial forgiveness would be L'il Bit's forgiving L'il Bit. L'il Bit as an adult looking at and understanding her complicity...."

Complicity? Here, quick, what's your answer — both characters require forgiveness because:

a) Peck says he can't help it
b) Peck says L'il Bit wanted it too
c) Peck gives L'il Bit gifts and teaches her to drive
d) Peck says he loves L'il Bit
e) All of the above

Extra credit question: whose viewpoint does e) reflect? Research thoroughly. Begin at www.nambla.org, website of the North American Man-Boy Love Association, a pedoscele lobbying group dedicated to the decriminalization of sex between adults and children via the repeal of all age-of-consent laws.

Am I suggesting that *How I learned to Drive* will spawn new pedosceles? No. But picture a jury who has just seen the play sitting in judgment on a pedoscele, say Feifel, who is protesting that this is his sexuality, that he loves the boy, or girl, or boys, or girls, or boys and girls — how have their perceptions been influenced? Picture the judge, fresh from the theatre where he and his wife have taken in the most celebrated play of the season, picture the judge at the V.I.P. cocktail party with the producer, director, cast, and playwright. Think of this judge who must sentence this man.

In her A.R.T. interview Vogel says that it was important to give the audience a catharsis because, "Catharsis purges the pity and the terror and enables the audience to transcend them." Although I think in this case she is confusing catharsis with a happy ending (love, healing, forgiveness), I'm more concerned with the idea that what a playwright dealing with this material intends is for the audience to transcend the pity and the terror. Such transcendence requires of the audience nothing but the shaking of heads, the wringing of hands, and the helpless clucking of tongues which seem to be the usual repertoire of middle-class moral responses to atrocity. This is a far cry from tragedy. Maybe we can't have tragedy in American theater. Maybe audiences will not tolerate the truth. We used to know that incest was a tragedy.

Until rather recently it was impossible to talk about the sexual abuse of children. Today we can talk about it — and talk about it and talk about it! — but only if certain rules are followed, certain shibboleths honored, certain phrases, as if ritual, uttered. We have to talk about "the cycle of abuse" which, of course, places responsibility precisely nowhere. We have to cast the issue as a matter of sexuality, not violence (which, by the way, abets homophobes and erotophobes who would have all sexual relationships heterosexual, married [preferably in their church], and man-on-top.) We have to talk about love, healing, and forgiveness.

That is, unless you prefer outrage, action, and the protection of children. Unless you prefer justice. Unless you would like things to change.

A POET'S PROGRESS: READING ROBERT GIBBONS

> Who among us has not dreamt of a particular prose, a poetic prose which could translate the lyrical movements of the mind, the undulations of reverie, the leaps of conscience?
>
> — Baudelaire

IN HIS ESSAY "Training For Poets," H. L. Hix writes, "Poetic inspiration occurs not upon the occasion of an unmotivated visit from a capricious muse but as a function of the poet's own progressive embodiment of an attitude toward language and the world." I would like to trace Robert Gibbons' development across three decades of publication with Hix's statement in mind.

To read Gibbons feels like learning to read the world again, as one does in early childhood, continually making connections — some sound, some spurious — among the things one is learning. There is a radical innocence here — not of the Craig Raine *What-If-You-Were-A-Martian?* school, but a less studied and manufactured naked looking, more related to Emerson's "transparent eyeball" than to any willed suppression of the foreknown. There is, in this poet now a grandfather, still a boyish intelligence fully capable both of apprehending beauty afresh and — in his dissenting mode — pointing out that the emperor is without clothes. In fact, it is well to recall that the clothes being praised by all others in the Emperor's retinue are made of words, insincere by virtue of their intentional masking of reality, indeed of the reality of an absence — of beauty, of utility, of meaning. Gibbons is attempting nothing less than the restoral of what Baudrillard called "the dialectical capacity of representation as a visible and intelligible mediation of the Real."

In Baudrillard's schema, which he called "the precession of the simulacra," signs (words, images, poems, works of art) begin, at least ideally, as mirrors to reality, equivalents to experience. Soon, however, the sign begins to be used to mask a reality, and later to mask the absence of a reality (as in the example of the emperor's new clothes.) Finally, the sign becomes independent of reality, referring only to itself.

I don't mean to suggest for a minute that one needs Baudrillard's apparatus — or anyone else's — to read Gibbons. The worth of his revolutionary poetics, which I will trace here, does not depend on an academic taxonomy. His poems locate the real at the intersection of desire and history. Language, sullied by pandering and propaganda, is restored in this poet's work to a medium capable not only of art, but of reintegration, regaining its erotic relation, its ability to respond sensually, to the world.

Big claims; perhaps it can be argued that this is what poetry always attempts to do if it is genuine, to "purify the language of the tribe" in Yeats' formulation. But there are few poets in any generation who are able to keep this commitment at the heart of their work, and fewer who have understood this charge, especially in the wash from postmodernism's often intersecting wakes, in the way that Gibbons has embraced it in his work.

Gibbons approaches poetry not as a profession or career, but as a vocation; in as much as that term conjures a priestly identity that sets one apart, I expect that Gibbons, radical democrat that he is, would reject it. And yet his practice and his poems are one and the same and seem to arise from his embrace of the ontological category "poet." It is as if there is a form, platonic, *a priori*, to be bodied forth in time, as one bodies forth other ontological designations like father, mother, warrior, healer, leader, lover. To read Gibbons body of work from its beginnings to the present is to watch him make himself into a poet the way Coltrane or Mingus made themselves into musicians.

Gibbons began publishing his poems in a series of chapbooks in 1980. Small press publications, exquisitely designed, on cream stock, hand-sewn, these thin books are made with the same care as the poems themselves. The first of these, *Yellow & Black* (Four Zoas Night House), demonstrates Gibbons' equal interest in word and world, in where they meet, escorted there by the poet's commitment to precision, the words sometimes strange as the world is sometimes strange. Take the second stanza of the poem "The Scimitar Moon":

> The scimitar
> Moon
> slices through the
> chrysalis
> of the Earth's albedo
> delivering

a vision
cultivated
in the wild.

"Albedo" is the strange word here of course, but also the exact one; it means the electromagnetic "skin" on a celestial body as well as the thin membrane of white pulp lining the peel of a fruit. For this reader, that word unlocks the extended metaphor of the poem, a poem that begins the implicit enactment of Gibbons' poetic mission — delivering/ a vision/ cultivated/ in the wild — that will body forth in his subsequent work where his care for the visionary fruit beneath the rind of the world will require a commitment to remaining "in the wild." One thinks of Yeats' statement that "There is another world, but it is in this one."

Rereading the title poem with the hindsight afforded by familiarity with Gibbons' work, especially his most recent, one can see plainly the urge to trace connections historical and cultural in order to subvert compartmentalized understandings. This synthesizing urge, which refuses to dumb itself down or exclude any of the manifold things this learned poet knows, will be familiar to readers of Pound's *Cantos*, Olson's *Maximus Poems*, or Duncan's *Passages*. "Yellow & Black" recounts a trip to Mexico and an encounter there with a mosque containing a sculpted Black Christ crucified, a figure both soiled and sanctified by the dirty hands of the pious. I will quote part two of the poem here:

In March 1911, searching for the creators of African
glass, similar to that found in sites with terra-cottas
and bronzes in the Yoruba holy city of Ile-Ife,
Frobenius enters the craftsman quarter of Bida, Nigeria

with the Massaga Tribesmen, working in a guild system,
are manufacturing the glass in two indigenous colors
yellow and black, leading him to call the splendid
Past, the poem of related cultures

In a book otherwise filled with shapely lyrics, their movement and music largely the product of the tension between line and syntax, this poem, attempting to be faithful to the understanding that is its subject, appears to strain against lineation itself; indeed it is hard to determine if these are truly lines in the conventional sense or simply ragged right paragraphs. It may be too much to say this fullness prefigures Gibbon's eventual embrace of the prose poem, but I believe we can begin to see that the poet here is already pressed by his material to find a form capacious enough to accommodate its reach and allusiveness.

The Woman in the Paragraph (Cat Island Press, 1982) is comprised of 17 quiet, meditative, and observant short poems, including such lyric gems as "Winged Psyche", "Kouretes", and the exquisite epithalamion, "The Ring the Sun Is, The Silence in the Vow". Although Gibbons has spoken of the profound influence of Charles Olson's work on his development, Olson's student and colleague, Robert Creeley, seems more in evidence here. (In a recent interview, Gibbons acknowledges Olson's influence, as well as his own need to escape from it, "It took me a long time to get free.") However, citing Creeley's presence in these poems is not to suggest that they are at all derivative, it is rather to say that Gibbons is guided by the same insistence that form be the inevitable extension of content, the shapeliness of the idea emerging from contemplation of the subject itself. It is the beginning of his repudiation of prosodic artifice, a turning away that will be accomplished after a dozen more poems in free verse, the chapbook *Ardors* (Innerer Klang, 1986.)

The 12 poems of *Ardors* worry the question "What is color?" and avail themselves even more fully than before of the poet's love and knowledge of the visual arts. (Gibbons was, for a time, a librarian at The National Gallery.) More than that, they discover, via this steady inquiry, the "ardors" of the title. The first lines of "Light of a Dark River", the first poem in the book, make a chord that will be heard in various keys throughout the sequence:

> There is no grief
> without cause of Love

Composed in graceful free verse couplets, Gibbons' verse here has the effect of slowing our movement through the sequence, encouraging a savoring of detail. As we progress, we note recurring words, images, lines ("A rich light endures the distance which is night.") And we approach, with a kind of musical hesitance, a moment of insight, part memory, part family lore, in which the poet sees himself as a feverish child:

> My first memory occurred two miles
>
> from there, a lambent sun at night
> appeared above French doors to decorate,
>
> I was later told by those attendant,
> the recurring fever of a four year old.

I may be taking too much time discussing this early work, but when a poet is at once as *sui generis* and as informed by aesthetic theory and the practice of his (claimed, honored) forbears, it seems well to try to trace his progress toward the full and confident embrace of the poetic project he has chosen to make his inheritance and responsibility.

Lover, Is This Exile? (Innerer Klang, 1989) seems to me the breakthrough work of Gibbons' early career; for one thing, it marks his departure from verse, for another, he has broken the bonds of the merely personal self, and audaciously so:

> *This narrator earth, lines wrested from the block & pigment of truth. The point at which the glare of objects enters directly & in their most solid forms surge into our own lives, from an oblique angle others march in: the erotic equal of the body itself.*

reads the italic proem that sets the sequence in motion. The whole chapbook is bathed in the light of the understanding set forth here, in fact the rest of Gibbons' work in its entirety seems to me to proceed from this "point at which the glare of objects enters directly," and his poetic practice will be to abide there, or try to, where the world shows itself to be "the erotic equal of the body itself," where "others march in" so that there is a kind of spiritual commerce rooted in a shared erotic reality.

In other words, Gibbons is a poet less concerned with forging a stance toward the world of experience than one committed to finding a poetics that will help him remain present, as fully as possible, within it. This is a positioning of the spirit that keeps him in the doorway Janus-like, looking both out and in, where the poet does not so much exist in relation to his world as he both contains it in an expanded consciousness and lives inside its rhythms. His stance is less reciprocal than complementary, to borrow Gregory Bateson's terms; he does not "relate to" the world so much as situate himself within its bounty, its hungers, and its suffering, its fundamentally erotic reality. To enumerate the ways that such work is healing, reparative, we would have to discuss the Cartesian error, or perhaps before that the shift in human consciousness attendant to the Neolithic change from hunting to agriculture, or perhaps to the Fall itself, the ancient "exile" of the title.

Any poet who pursues a vision, who intuits a direction to take, must find a way to break with the period style. Today's emphasis on "craft," on the poem as a made object, admits of only so much innovation, after all. Gibbons' attempt to reflect in his writing the way he wishes to be radically present has led him to a technique, a practice that Whitman describes at the beginning of *Specimen Days*:

> If I do it at all I must delay no longer. Incongruous and full of skips and jumps... All bundled up and tied by a big string, the resolution and indeed mandate comes to me this day, this hour, — (and what a day! What an hour just passing! the luxury of riant grass and blowing breeze, with all the shows of sun and sky and perfect temperature, never before so filling me, body and soul), — to go home untie the bundle, reel-out diary scraps and memoranda, just as they are, large or small, one after another, into print-packages, and let the mélange's lackings and wants of connection take care of themselves. It will illustrate one phase of humanity anyhow. How few of life's days and hours (and they not by relative value or proportion, but by chance) are ever noted.

Whitman is falsely modest here, but he is doubtless right in claiming that his method arose from necessity, and his achievement in that book is to render the life of his times as no one else has. I suspect that Whitman and Gibbons arrived at similar crossroads, where to remain whole and responsive to a furious reality (Whitman's Civil War, Gibbons' millennial landslide of global history and culture) it is necessary to respond at a rate coequal with the press of experience, or else begin to narrow one's aperture and live in a manner less welcoming to the world. I suppose that we can call this courage. From here on out, growing more and more confident and prolific, Gibbons continues to refine this method of bricolage, as if to refuse to deny any part of his experience. He also continues to question the common wisdom about poetry, its form and function. There will be no collections of little green monopoly house poems from him. It starts here, after a period of study and preparation, with *Lover, Is This Exile?* and continues as one long improvisation that leaves us two decades later with a portrait of an educated, lively, earthy, sensual, responsive, millennial man and his times — our times.

I should mention that I come to this writing as one who for years professed skepticism regarding the prose poem. Sometimes my objection was to the term — how distinguish the prose poem from the short-short? From "flash" forms? Other times prose poems seemed to me the first paragraphs of narratives the writer hadn't the energy, art, or inclination to pursue. I would have agreed with the critic Stephen Yenser: "the distinction between *poetry* and *verse* is a facile distinction, and *prose poem* is a contradiction in terms." That was, of course, before reading Gibbons who seems to me to have successfully enacted the injunction of his idol, Baudelaire: "Always be a poet; even in prose."

Of DC (Innerer Klang, 1992), with a cover designed by the artist Robert Rauschenberg, continues the ongoing metamorphosis of the poet, along with his strengthening confidence that he can break free of other compositional habits. "As if it were all informative, signaling, with the added dynamic of sensuous appreciation. Non-interpretive, no mere looking for that which is analogous," he writes in "Sentences for Wisteria," reminding himself that he is alive in the world, at a particular complex instant; he does not raid the world to plunder it for analogies. The practice that I see him defining and refining for himself is akin to that of Eliade's primitive nomads carrying with them a pole that is the Axis Mundi so that wherever they stop they can erect it and know where the center of the world is. For Gibbons, that world center will move from DC to Boston to Gloucester, to Paris, to Venice, and to Portland, Maine, all places which he has found to be "the erotic equal of the body itself."

This Vanishing Architecture (Innerer Klang, 2001) is an exquisite series of poems that offer variations on three ideas, from Kristeva, Colette, and Proust that comprise the chapbook's epigraph:

> *Remembering through the senses is the same as being in love, & these two processes constitute the narrator's [Proust's] essence. Venice — the place made of the same substance as the narrator's desire.*
>
> — *Kristeva*

> *For anyone not able to dawdle along a pavement & indulge the fortuitous whims & luck of the stroller, there remain only the superficial sights. There is always so much to look at when one travels slowly.*
>
> — *Colette*

> *Church steeples or wild grass growing in a wall — they composed a magical scrawl, complex & elaborate, their essential character was that I was not free to choose them, as such they were given to me.*
>
> — *Proust*

By the time we arrive at this series of poems, Gibbons has wholly embraced the more ample and accommodating form of the prose poem, and his method, his practice becomes truly his own. Take for example the second part of "Twin to the Campanile in Venice":

> When my two young friends and I took a tour of the Custom House in Boston, twin to the campanile in Venice, I thought of the blue beginning Visconti gives Aschenbach's arrival by steamer, the bewildered hero seated in a rattan deck chair, belltower ultimately visible in the pink distance. Aschenbach could well be Proust's coalheaver, who denies he is one, although he's black all over. This week the winged-lion of the Chadwick Lead Works on High St. said, as I stood under its paws, "I may not rival St. Mark's, but I'm present for you."

The allusiveness here is associative, not decorative or studied, and its consequence is the restoration of history, art, film, literature, symbol, and architecture as the true context for our daily life. That there is more to an encounter, a photograph, a streetscape, or a memory then we at first realize is a given for this poet, as is the radical subjectivity, the self that is the spider to all this webwork.

Here the New World resembles the Old, is in fact a knock-off of it. And the "Death in Venice" referred to is not Mann's story but Visconti's film version of it. An observation about the protagonist Aschenbach's likeness to "Proust's coalheaver" further raises the issues of similitude, dissimulation, and denial. This allusiveness is extended to the transmigration of the winged lion (who speaks!) "Of the Chadwick Lead Works on High Street" who both evokes and denies the St. Mark's original (itself, it should be pointed out, an emblem of Assyrian origin) in the way of old wine in new bottles, bringing us full circle to the New World's denial of the Old, the recurrence of archetypal motifs, and the arguable superiority by default of whatever is "present for you."

One caveat about my own close reading here, which perhaps misleadingly approaches allegory: Gibbons is not so didactic as to play algebraic games with what the world affords him; it runs counter to his method, even at this still early articulation of his vision. And yet there is excitement in the connections he makes across cultures, through centuries. The poet Susan Tichy has remarked of collage that it is a "nest" in that it is constructed of things removed from their earlier contexts and brought together for a new purpose. In a Gibbons prose poem, which seems to have as much in common with Andy Goldsworthy as with Baudelaire or St. John Perse, the instant is an instance of something breaking through to consciousness, some apprehension of relation, and there are few prose fasteners, the elements plaited together with no more rhetoric than is necessary to keep them in relation to one another.

To remain for the moment with "Twin to the Campanile in Venice," consider the first paragraph —the poem is in two — which moves from "artillery Brown" Belgrade to a view of Venice from the air that calls to mind a drawing by Jacopo de Barberi in 1500, as well as a recent dream of the poet. These associational "leaps" feel synaptic, not strategic or crafty. There is happily something of the essayist in Gibbons' work, and I mean that in the purest sense, the credo from which Montaigne proceeded, that everything in the universe is connected to everything else. Associative power is honored, and recognized as not only the individual consciousness showing itself, but at least some of the time, the still living patterns of history, culture, and psychology emerging into view. *This Vanishing Architecture* ends with the poem "The Present Is The Roof Of Time" in which a flower girl (herself a kind of avatar) balances "flattened cardboard boxes that about an hour before, millennia before, contained gladioli, irises, strawberries, oranges, roses, yes a living caryatid, the long bodily architectonic column of Time." From this point onward, as if Gibbons has written himself to the vantage he will take thereafter, Time is capitalized, a kind of piety that suggests that the poet has found and made explicit his Daemon.

In 2004, Six Gallery Press published Gibbons' first two full-length books, *Streets for Two Dancers* and *The Book of Assassinations*, within a month of each other. Here, from the former, is "Communicating Vessels":

> It was as if things & utterance merged. Red delphinium vibrated behind our talk influenced by French Burgundy. The friend called soul and fertility of soil equal. It happened in a flash. On a street given over almost entirely to fashion. For a second poetry clasped presence and memory together with the strength of sinew. Language, direct descendent of the senses. Love rose, a sea in the bloodstream.

a poem which seems to me an explicit ars poetica, as well as the record of one of those instances for which Gibbons works so hard to be eligible, those moments when the world inside this one, a world elemental, archetypal and unchanging, shows through: "It happened in a flash. On a street given over almost entirely to fashion."

In *The Book of Assassinations* the poet continues to question the means by which we are able to make poetry, indeed to make meaning. In "About American Poetry" Gibbons makes his case explicitly for a responsive rather than willful poetics, quoting himself quoting Olson at a symposium, "The trouble with the symbol is, it does not trouble."

Baudelaire, whose photograph is on the cover, is the presiding spirit of *The Book of Assassinations*, also providing two of the four epigraphs; the first of these, however, is Walter Benjamin's: "Let no thought pass incognito, and keep your notebook as strictly as the authorities keep their register of aliens." What follows is 137 pages of poetry, 103 poems. So what's happened? Has our poet become a mere diarist? Yes and no: there is no "mere" about it after such a long and learned cultivation of both oneself and the means at hand. We are well to recall that the root of journal means day, and that Gibbons daily genuflects to Time, working to remain open to all it brings.

Poets' journals are generally understood to be a secondary literary pleasure, part gossip mongering, part investigation of creativity, part research into the poet's life and times — a pleasure mainly enjoyed by scholars and biographers. Still, interested readers may search there for the sources of the poet's inspiration, or for keys to the poet's practice: how did he or she transform the dross of experience to the value of art?

But what of the poet who makes the journal itself, with its disciplined observations of both the inner and outer world, his art? In this case, the interval between experience and reconsideration represents also the space between candor and self-portrayal, a kind of "what you see is what you get." Honesty raised, or restored, to its place as a primary virtue. The cost to the poet, or at least to the poet's ego, must be enormous.

Read in the aggregate, *Body Of Time* and *Beyond Time: New & Selected Work 1977-2007* are a kind of memoir, or anti-memoir insofar as there is no attempt to create a story, that offer a portrait of millennial man as open, as naked, as welcoming to experience, as possible. Indeed, one of the poems in *Body of Time* seems to address this specifically, even in its title, "How Much More Alive Can A Man Be"? An exemplary poem, it can stand here to represent some of the deep pleasures of moving in this poet's mind with him as he invites us to do:

How Much More Alive Can A Man Be?

> One of those mundane Mondays when one might as well be interred, or disinterred, for that matter. Everything so familiar, nothing stands out. Then Claire writes from Pittsburgh that stone heads above Roman doors convey welcome & demarcation; David wonders from London if I've seen the Medusas placed sideways to avoid the Pagan evil eye in the basilica cistern in Istanbul; & by pure chance, a couple of hours later, Itir writes from her cousin's house on the Asian side of the city that I wouldn't believe the voluptuousness of the Virgin Tower in the middle of the Bosporus, while watching the sunset on the European side of Istanbul. Suddenly I'm lifted up, risen by tension carved in stone in Rome, & by the generous hand that wrote it. Far, far from immune to the power of the evil eye, poets are able to avert that gaze by inversion of ego toward creativity, & the love of the language of fellow men. How much more alive can a man be, when out of the mundane of every

> day, a Virgin surfaces out of narrow straits linking Black and Mamara Seas, illuminated by a Byzantine-neon light, & quiet, humble tongue?

Body of Time is a treasury of tesserae, sharp shards of what can never be in this time-bound life apprehended whole, but which consciousness can arrange and rearrange kaleidoscopically in a kind of ecstatic acknowledgment, almost worship, of ongoingness, of Gibbons' ever capitalized "Time."

The individual prose poems of *Body Of Time* accrue to what Claire Barbetti calls, in her preface to that volume, "the massive surface of a corpus witnessing itself through language." Like the poet's friend Gang's Buddhist wish to be reincarnated as a stone "in my best friends pocket" ("A Small Stone",) the poet wants only that ecstasy that will further unify him with the rest of creation. In "To An Already Grace Filled Day," he watches a kingfisher watching with presumed hunger a school of minnows in shallow water. "Now it's on the next rock over," he writes, "larger than I thought through my binoculars. Both with our work cut out for us." Gibbons has all he can do to simply perceive, to witness the terrible beauty of this one visible world. If the occult, the hidden, the transcendent nevertheless appears, it is through the power and patience of his looking, his capturing the visible. He knows there is "One star visible, & a billion burning." ("The Right Stone") and that he can only examine the one that Time presents to him, visible and subject to his questioning and appreciation.

Reading the poems of *Body of Time* page after page is to experience a torrent of images, allusions, ideas, questions, conversations, meals, journeys, homecomings, dissident outrage, and outpourings of love and appreciation for the poet's beloved, Kathleen. And yet this is a flood somehow not of water and earth, leaving a residue, but of air and light, leaving energy.

What we see and what we get from Robert Gibbons in his later work, *Travels Inside The Archive* is something like time lapse photography whereby we see themes, thoughts, questions, allegiances, outrage, regrets, epiphanies — and above all observations — amounting to the shape of a consciousness with that generosity of attention Whitman called "amative-ness;" indeed, these are truly Gibbons' own *Specimen Days*. There is more of the world in these poems, seen through the poet's daily gaze at his beloved city of Portland, Maine, than in any since *Leaves of Grass*. (One epigraph to this work is indeed from Whitman: "City of my walks and joys!") An index of this volume, the record of one year's daily improvisations, from November 24th, 2007 to November 24th, 2008, would be nearly as long as the book itself. The 986 foot tanker Polar Adventure, Mayakovsky, Robert Frank, Thelonious Monk, Benazir Bhutto, varieties of wine, fish, — and always Gibbons' ongoing Rubaiyat, his celebration of Kathleen's companionship. His literary reference points alone include Benjamin, Kristeva, Ranciere, Baudelaire, Pound, Olson, Kerouac, Rilke, Cixous, Celan, Lorca, Deleuze, Vallejo, and others. The book is complexly prismatic. It is as if, at bottom, his aim is, roughly stated: these things all exist together in Time, in which and of which I am conscious, therefore allowing them — ships, books, memories, fish, water, persons, sky — to move, to exist in dynamic relation in language on the page, is the way to chronicle both the inner and outer world's continual shifting, becoming, turning and returning.

Gibbons is not a religious poet in any conventional sense; however, there is something of the responsiveness of a devout adherent in the discipline that so faithfully produced this book. To say this work is *re-ligious* is only to suggest it is re-joining, reparative, reunifying. Gibbons is a poet of the day; seldom do the nocturnal humors of melancholy, regret, sadness, wistfulness, or ennui intrude. The sun shines in his poems — on the waves of the harbor, the ships from far ports, the conversations, the books and paintings and architecture, the travel, the food and wine, the commerce of a world brave and new each day. His genius is for freshness, for somehow renewing the sense of wonder.

And yet to acknowledge the diurnal nature of his work is not to suggest a lack of shade, of shadow. Many of the poems in *Travels Inside The Archive* are overcast and darkened by a political anger, by foreboding, by umbrage at the latest instance of barbarism. Here is "Possible Swift Solution?":

> Monday, September 22, 2008
>
> It may not be a bad idea, necessarily, regarding a few thieves on Wall Street, or butchers in government, to follow a precedent set by folk near Goya's hometown in Zaragoza, which the artist recorded in a drawing & eye witness account jotted down in his *Album F.* Goya says the people of the town placed a constable named Lampinos inside the body of a dead horse, & left him there overnight to die. He survived the night, while dogs circled the carcass gobbling up discarded entrails. Now, I'm not suggesting we allow the dogs of Abu Ghraib in, & I'm not at all suggesting death result. Just a little *YouTube* excerpt of thieves, butchers, & advocates of torture sewn

> inside the belly of an already dead nag, their heads, as Goya drew it, peeking out of the rear end, names of CEO's & Administration officials running in bold print underneath?

I have wondered what accounts for Gibbons' obscurity, the ignorance of his work among readers of contemporary poetry. Is it because his entire body of work has been published by small or independent presses? Is it because the prose poem is seen as a lesser form? Does the fact that, despite his immense erudition, Gibbons has never held a faculty position in a university account for it? Or could it be that the sheer volume of his output — close to a thousand new poems in the last decade — suggests, wrongly, (since we often confuse rarity with value) that there can be little of worth there? Or are other poets, comprising these days the bulk of poetry's readership, simply intimidated? I don't know.

I do know that by any measure, these are poems that deliver. If we bring Aristotle's simple criteria to bear on them, we find they delight us with their adventurous juxtapositions, their hunches and intuitions, their improvisatory and unpredictable movements, and they instruct us, not because the poems are didactic but because the poet's erudition is the result of his indefatigable curiosity and his only pedagogical impulse is to share with enthusiasm what he discovers. It is a combination of virtues Theodore Roethke would have recognized. "A teacher," Roethke wrote, "is one who carries on his education in public."

Still, I suspect that Gibbons doesn't care much about his reputation. He's been doing what he does, and doing it better and better, for thirty years, as if in agreement with Milton that the poet "ought himselfe to bee a true poeme." Gibbons is. And serious readers deserve to know his work. To read Gibbons, to situate yourself at the proper angle to his work, is to feel a chthonic rumbling, as if tectonic shifts are occurring under you as you allow your mind to move with his. Because his philosophical orientation is more and more strongly an articulation of an alternative to the common wisdom, and perhaps of a more salutary way of being in the world, we read him with a quickening sense of excitement akin to danger, as if we are being summoned to let go, to come away, to accompany the poet on something like Whitman's Open Road.

POETRY IS DISSENT

POETRY IS POLITICAL. Period. It has often been remarked that the so-called "apolitical" poem, the objet d'art, is of course political in its acceptance of the status quo. But while I agree with that view, that's not quite what I'm getting at here. I believe poetry is political because a poet is always both working with and straining against language. That may seem like a truism, and you may ask "What's political about that?" Well, for starters, the question of what to accept about how the world is represented in words, and what to reject. In some respects it is a poet's duty to reject the verbal and rhetorical formulations of his or her moment in time. In other words, a poet is always on a quest for originality, which is not a question of trying not to sound like anyone else, a question of what these days is called "branding," but a return to the great storehouse of language, to see what can be found there that is useful and true to this moment. The part of me engaged in that process is the oldest part of me — or maybe I should say the youngest since I started doing it before I can remember anything else.

As a child, words come from a world that was there before you arrived, and you presume, because you must, that there is some correlation between the words and the things and actions and qualities for which they stand. This is the original suspension of disbelief required to acquire language in the first place. And then you go about choosing among the words offered. You try to match the right one with the right thing. You try to say it correctly. You test out the words on other people, usually your parents. Sometimes they think you're cute, other times they threaten to wash out your mouth with soap!

But soon enough and before you're even aware of it, you are toughening your spirit on the successive disappointments that you suffer as you learn, again and again, that the words are inadequate. You must find new ones, or combine them in a new way. Many, if not most people, make some peace with the inadequacy of language. I think what makes a person a poet (whether they write in verse or prose) is an abiding commitment to try again, all the while knowing that it is in the nature of language, and of the essence of the whole enterprise, that you will fail.

This is, at heart, a moral commitment, or so I believe, because one of the reasons words have come to disappoint has to do with their deliberate misuse, with their having been poisoned by dishonesty. Here is where I could rant about the ubiquity of advertisers' and politicians' designs on us, but it is enough, I think, to simply make the point.

Let me give you a favorite poem of mine, by the great Polish poet Zbigniew Herbert, as a way of describing the act, the ethical and political act, of writing poetry:

A Knocker

by Zbigniew Herbert
translated by Czeslaw Milosz and Peter Dale Scott

There are those who grow
gardens in their heads
paths lead from their hair
to sunny and white cities

it's easy for them to write
they close their eyes
immediately schools of images
stream down from their foreheads

my imagination
is a piece of board
my sole instrument
is a wooden stick

I strike the board
it answers me
yes—yes
no—no

for others the green bell of a tree
the blue bell of water
I have a knocker
from unprotected gardens

I thump on the board
and it prompts me
with the moralist's dry poem
yes—yes
no—no

Maybe in another time, a time when the world had not been poisoned by a century of genocides and mechanized murder, and before the continuing threat of ecocide, a poet could trust his or her culture's assumptions about what it means to be good, or powerful, or heroic, or simply human. We do not live in a time like that. And so, we are "moralists" or ought to be, as Herbert unapologetically suggests he is. But it is not the finger-wagging moralism of the self-righteous Herbert's talking about here; it is instead the weighing of words, and a rigorous attention to how these same words have been used before. Because the discourses of the past have brought us to a sorry spiritual state, we can take nothing for granted, nor can we be silent.

Here's a recent poem of my own — not great, way too simple, but least short — that asks a similar question about the poet's relation to the received world:

Perplexity

In my seventh decade
I have not been able to decide
if we have made a mess of everything

because we have turned away
from what the old stories, poems, rituals
sought to preserve by teaching us,

or if we've learned those lessons all too well.

Though I've railed against Caesar
and raged against the gods,

I am still unable to decide.

If poets do not fear the misrepresentation of the world, if we do not guard against it, work against it hunched over the page or keyboard, then what are we doing? What is being accomplished, and whom does it serve?

It seems to me that poets are of little value who aren't trying to see through the fog of stereotypes, untruths, half-truths, and alienating narratives that profit a few at the expense of the rest of us. How do we address the racism, or racialized oppression, that has deeply injured our ability to see one another clearly in America? Why should we continue, as writers, to acquiesce in our own infantilization, as if literature were a playground where what happens is of no consequence in the world?

Here's how the post-WWII critic George Steiner put it ". . . any thesis that would, either theoretically or practically, put literature and the arts beyond good and evil is spurious. The archaic torso in Rilke's famous poem says to us 'change your life'. So does any poem, novel, play, painting, musical composition, worth meeting."

And yet, without beauty — in the case of poetry the satisfying and pleasurable play of language, the bodily, erotic tongue caressing the thrilled ear, the soul remains asleep while the intellect goes on chewing its flavorless daily bread. I'm reminded of Yeats' comment that some poets have pulpits but no altars and others have altars but no pulpit — his version of Aristotle's charge to the poet to both "delight and instruct." The temptation is to try to oppose the pulpit-less deco-poets by leaning way out over your own pulpit with an excoriating index finger in the air. But the real alternative is to enact the poem in beauty's sanctuary, the heart thereby opened to hear words that challenge, inform, and refresh us in the struggle for a just future.

Far from being a luxury, poetry is the essential medium. It is because poetry is handmade, because it does not require a great deal of money to perform its artistry and effect its influence, that it can save us. Most people find poets archaic, quaint, maybe charming, like candle-light. But think how useful candles are when the power goes out. And think about the gathering storm, and the darkness that has begun to fall.

PROCEDURE: A Look Inside

For William Orem

NOT LONG AGO, I saw either my death, the very shape of it, or else the dark outline of my fear. Maybe they're one and the same. I cannot read a flouroscope, but when I craned my neck from my fetal position on the icy metal table and saw a black shape among the billowy barium-illumined folds of my insides, a jagged twist of fear shot through my chest and my heart began to pound.

Over and over I told myself that the dark form, something like a footprint, was no doubt a normal shadow, but my fear remained. I tried to read the looks, the gestures, the rhythms of the technician and his assistant: surely if they had seen my death in there, hiding like a rat, they would betray their fear or pity somehow. But they were busy, the technician reassuring me with his practiced patter – "just a few more moments, you're doing fine, you're doing fine," and his assistant chirpy as a real estate agent. Impenetrable, their behavior was no easier to read than the round screen where I'd seen the murky tread of my own mortality.

What if I'd been less inhibited? What if I'd cried out, "Jesus, what the hell is that?" What would they have answered? I wish I had not looked, but how could I not?

After I dressed, I was served juice and crackers. I wanted to ask — of course I did — but the technician preempted that and, frankly, I was a little relieved. "Your doctor will be in touch with you when he's interpreted the results."

Driving home, stopped at a red light, I noted that I'd already begun talking to myself in the stoic's voice I've used occasionally when faced with a loved one's frightening hospital stay, or at a bedside vigil when death was inescapable. Death *is* a normal shadow, I told myself; I've just trained myself, like the rest of us, to ignore it. I began to wonder at how much of what we call our daily lives is perhaps a vast conspiracy in which we all take part, a contract we have with one another to play our various roles, all to distract us from that dark shape, to keep us sheltered from what I'd glimpsed — inside me! — and was still trying to absorb.

In addition to the stoical view, but not occluding or softening it, was another, more spiritual perspective. It sounds trite to call it a lesson in humility, but that's what it was. I was tiny and soft, a mealworm or a slug, a dust mote, a random speck of nearly nothing.

The stoic again took the upper hand: If there was a fight ahead, I told myself, I would try to be worthy of it; if resignation was called for, I would try to accept my sentence with dignity.

But soon I found I was accusing myself of having wasted time, of squandering what life I'd been vouchsafed, now that it might be nearly over. Was that because I had not sufficiently valued it? Because I did not know how best to live it? Because I had somehow transgressed? Such are the self-flagellations of a cradle Catholic. And I suspect my insistence on some level of personal responsibility was an assertion of my own authority: I must have caused it; I am a sinner. But it's alright, the thinking goes, because we are all sinners and, being human, all we can do is ask forgiveness. I didn't ask forgiveness, though; I just appreciated the elegant psychological slipknot I'd just executed, a metaphysical maneuver I now saw clearly, feeling thankful to those who taught me how to do it. Our need to at least feel in control of what is beyond control requires us to blame ourselves for nearly everything that befalls us, but the universality of that predicament excuses us, so long as we acknowledge it and are willing to be judged as "only human" and forgiven. It was hardly an accident that I'd employed this half-hitch and loop when I felt most vulnerable, tiny, and inconsequential.

I was lost in these metacognitive musings, successfully in flight from my fear, when the light changed and, impatient, the guy behind me leaned on his horn, slamming me back in my body and scaring the living crap out of me.

I wasn't worried about what my body would do with this intruder lurking in my bowels; my body would fight as it had been trained to do by aeons of evolution. It would either win or lose against its opponent. It knew what to do, and I would make sure that it had the best medical allies in that contest. No, my mind would be the arena in which I had to fight, where defeat would mean despair and meaninglessness and misery. I began to see that my parents and teachers, my culture and religious training, had afforded me multiple perspectives, taught me to plead my case for meaning on multiple grounds, to embrace various premises, as if I'd been given a wide shelf of books to take down and read from as needed. The books didn't need to agree; they only needed, each of them, to suffice for the moment. I felt grateful for this insulation from terror and madness. I felt well-equipped.

I still think it's odd, though, that in the days after, waiting for my test results, not once, not for a single moment, did I entertain the idea of an afterlife. I remained plenty scared, though hiding it from others helped me put it from my mind for hours at a time. I considered my absence and its impact on my wife, my grown children, friends, colleagues, students. I thought of work I wanted to accomplish. I thought of things I needed to do and people I needed to speak to while I still had the chance. I started making lists: people to forgive; people to ask for forgiveness; people to thank. I even thought about what I would like done with my remains. The prospect of a waiting paradise or a terrible punishment never crossed my mind, however; no other world awaited me, I felt sure.

But this world, finite, was never more real to me than it was that week — those seven days, those 10,000 minutes or so — awaiting the phone call from my PCP. It's hard to recapture, now that my anxiety has eased, that weird penumbra fear had bestowed on even the most familiar things.

REMEMBERING THE ALCHEMISTS

> The children are always ours, every single one of them, all over the globe; and I am beginning to suspect that whoever is incapable of recognizing this may be incapable of morality.
>
> — James Baldwin

IN THE PAPER THERE was a photo of police on their hands and knees, crawling in the high grass beside a playground named for a little boy killed there by gunshot a few years earlier. They were looking for a more recent shell-casing, however, still unfound two days after the shot that struck a 10 year-old girl whose aunt had brought her there to climb and swing.

In the photo, the faces of the officers seemed desperate, as if they needed to find the shell-casing to save the little girl, who was then in critical condition at Children's Hospital. Their features suggested they might bring the casing to the hospital where a doctor would remove the pellets from the child's body, tamp them back into the casing, poke it back into the barrel of the shotgun, put it back into the hand of the young man full of rage who had pulled the trigger and stop him so that the aunt could stand behind her niece on the swing, giving her a push at intervals, her hand on the small of the child's back, careful not to push her too high.

In fact, by the time the photo was published the child was already gone; the doctors only waiting for her family to sign the papers to remove her from life support.

I've been trying to recall the first time I heard the word bullet. I have a snapshot of myself at age three or four aiming a toy pistol at the camera (probably my father was taking the picture.) "Pow! Pow! Pow!" I would have said, not having mastered, yet, the *a capella* imitations of gunfire that accompanied our make-believe combat. We didn't yet have a television to watch the cowboys shoot at the Indians, the soldiers shoot at one another, the cops shoot at the bank robbers, so we didn't know yet how a gun really sounded. When we did finally get a TV, I was especially proud of learning to make the sound of a bullet when it ricochets off a rock you're hiding behind: you make a good gunshot sound, lots of spit behind your front teeth, and then you add a little whistle at the end.

I used to take the foil wrappers from my mother's cigarette packages and roll them into what I meant to be silver bullets for my six-shooter because The Lone Ranger used only silver bullets in his Colt .45 so he could stop the bad guys without killing them. Like the virtuous masked man, I didn't want to kill anybody. I only wanted to be a hero, mysterious, on a white horse.

Bullet is a strange word. I used to picture a little bull in the dark, at the beginning of a long tunnel, stomping head down in its stall, waiting to charge into daylight and gore its victim — man, woman, beast, child. But no, the dictionary says it was once spelled bollet, a small round boll or ball, especially a cannon-ball.

When I was eight or maybe nine years old, I had two silver six-shooters, cap-pistols that shot red paper rolls of caps, that I kept in the holsters of a toy gun belt embossed with cow horns, horses, lariats, and other Western icons. I tied them to my thighs at the bottom because that's what gunfighters did so they could draw quickly. We used to have competitions in my neighborhood to see who was the fastest draw. I learned to twirl my guns before slipping them back in their holsters, sometimes pretending first to blow the smoke from their barrels.

Life imitates art. It follows that bad art begets bad lives. It's a safe bet that without the continual refreshment of our fatal ballistic romance, our obsession with guns would have long passed away, a relic of pioneer days, like the Conestoga wagon or buckskin britches. But the gun has been front and center in American film and television since we have had film and television. It's product placement hiding in plain sight. And it ensures bad art because it serves storytellers as the most common and simplistic deus ex machina of all: *Bang! You're dead.* Even worse: *Bang! Justice!*

A friend of mine, a poet and psychologist, wrote an essay about men and sexual violence for *The Good Men Project*, an online journal that claims some three million visitors a month and whose tagline is *The conversation no one else is having*. Midway through his essay, an ad appeared for the chance to win a free pistol, the latest US Army certified Sig Sauer, "The Military's First New Handgun in the Last 1/3 of a Century Delivers Reliability, Force and Spot On Accuracy Right Out of the Box."

When I alerted my friend, he couldn't see it. I don't mean that he couldn't see grounds for my dismay, I mean that he couldn't see the ad itself. It seems that an advertising algorithm had determined that I was a likely target (and yes, I intend the irony of that term.) Now, if the pitch had been for a fountain pen or even a hair-growing gel, I'd understand it as the latest in savvy marketing, but I have never owned a gun since I twirled that cap pistol, have no desire to own one, and otherwise prefer paperclips to ammo clips, literary magazines to 30-round magazines, and ploughshares to swords across the board.

So what does it mean that I am nonetheless a mark for a gun monger? Is it simple spillover, a supersaturation of advertising? Was the algorithm looking for sites that contain the word "men" or that have a male readership? But my friend did not receive the same ad. He inquired about it with the editors. They told him they had little control over the ads on their site, that they were selected by a third party with whom they had contracted.

What does it mean that one would never, ever, find an ad like that in a "women's magazine?" Well, for one thing, it points to the relationship between masculinity as we currently define it and destruction. It suggests that real men can be identified by their power to reorder the world by means of lethal violence. In this version of masculinity, not every man needs to actually inflict violence or bodily harm to be considered suitably masculine (which also means, in this discourse, heterosexual) but there has to be at least some signaling that he is willing to do so. Or maybe it's enough simply to not object to this weird definition of manhood. Maybe it's enough to keep your mouth shut.

But let's truly have it, the conversation no one else is having: Is it normal that every day more than a million Americans pack their lunches and heigh-ho heigh-ho go off to work manufacturing increasingly efficient instruments that have no other purpose but the killing of other human beings? Well, yes, it is, has become, normal. The question is whether or not it is acceptable. And so far the answer seems to be yes.

Somehow a combination of economic pressure, rhetorical dishonesty, and a corporate culture similar across industries has managed to hide the fact that America's paychecks are stained with blood, to hide it even from the people who assemble its killing machines. The companies make "integrated systems, products, and solutions," offer young people the opportunity to "make your future with us" or even claim to be "making the world a safer place." For most, the work is straightforward, assembly-line work, and the tedium is relieved by creating a social nexus that includes holiday parties, athletic teams, fund-drives for local charities, T-shirts, and ballcaps with the company logo. Most days there's a card to sign for somebody's birthday or engagement or baby shower: Congratulations!

In the early 1970's, with the exuberance and promise of the antiwar movement and counter-culture turning to disillusion, the poet Charles Simic asked the question I am circling here:

Poem Without A Title

I say to the lead
Why did you let yourself
Be cast into a bullet?
Have you forgotten the alchemists?
Have you given up hope
In turning into gold?

Nobody answers.
Lead. Bullet. With names
Such as these
The sleep is deep and long.

Recently the President of the United States vetoed bipartisan legislation forbidding the sale of arms to Saudi Arabia, which as I write this is conducting a genocidal war against the people of Yemen, largely with American arms manufactured by Raytheon, General Dynamics, General Electric, Boeing, Lockheed Martin, and other companies central to our economy. He followed this by appointing Raytheon's chief lobbyist Director of Defense, who was swiftly confirmed by congress. Nothing new in that, of course; indeed, this is business-as-usual, following most recently the examples of Dick Cheney and Donald Rumsfeld.

I know, I know — big news: the president is corrupt, the congress is craven — but are we willing to admit that killing people is America's business model? I know that putting it so bluntly will seem unfair to many, but consider that if you combine defense contractors and manufacturers of other weapons and munitions we are talking about a 90 billion dollar sector of our economy. What does it mean to be the foremost arms dealer in the world? The health of our American economy presently depends upon the murder of other human beings. How did we get here? When did we make this deal with the devil? How long have we been addicted to this poison?

The answer involves a mysterious figure known to few: Zachariah Basileos Zaharoff, sometimes referred to as "Zed Zed" after his scrawled "ZZ" signature. Born in 1849 in what is now Turkey, he was employed, at age 12, by the local fire brigade in Istanbul — as an arsonist. As a teen he became a procurer for the local brothel, a role he expanded to trafficking young girls and blackmailing the men to whom he sold them. The son of a merchant, Zaharoff learned not only how to buy cheap and sell dear, he also found ways to elude regulation of his enterprises by keeping all his accounts secret, a modus operandi he maintained for his entire life. Summoned to court in London for "export irregularities," he sought protection in Greece where, it seems, his career as a salesman of weaponry began with his exclusive contract to sell the first-ever truly automatic, deadly rapid-fire machine gun, the Maxim, and the first (not very reliable) submarine. Zaharoff made several trips to the US to contract with industrialists to provide them with "factory girls" from Ireland, and on one trip married a wealthy Philadelphia heiress, providing him an infusion of capital and, by the way, making him a bigamist since he was already married to an Englishwoman. As he consolidated his wealth, he found that his ability to exploit international tensions was more lucrative than any other enterprise, and he devised what has come to be known as *Le Systeme Zaharoff*: sell to the Greeks, then sell to the Turks, then sell to their enemies' enemies, sell to the Russians, create and monger fear for profit, stoke conflicts, provoke war, and furnish weapons to both sides.

And the profits were astonishing. Soon Zaharoff was consorting with kings and prime ministers, financing arms manufacturing and development, advising militaries on three continents and generally amassing a great fortune. His model's similarities to a straightforward protection racket clearly derive from his boyhood job as an arsonist in Istanbul.

As his clientele engaged in the butchery of the First World War, his power increased with his ability to tip the scales in the direction of one or another of the combatants. With the fortune Zaharoff amassed, he was able not only to buy immunity from several prosecutions, but even to endow a Chair named in his honor at Oxford, and later to have himself knighted. His conversion to respectability was ensured when he founded British Petroleum. Shortly before his death in 1936, he removed from his safe the relatively few records he had kept of his dealings and burned them. It would take a whole book, one written by a more talented investigator than I, to peel apart the many plies of exploitation, manipulation, greed, sycophancy, blackmail, deception, secrecy, and ulteriority that comprise the crooked route that ZedZed took to become Sir Basil Zaharoff. I can only say that the course of that journey has become a model, creating markets, setting standards, creating norms, and generally poisoning the ethical understandings of our era. The deadly plume of oil purling from his BP's disastrous rig in the Gulf of Mexico offers a ready metaphor for this toxic history.

I was born in the middle of the 20th century, in the immediate aftermath of the bloodiest war in human history, with 80 million people slain, and the development of the most nightmarish weapons the world has ever known, weapons with the capacity to make every apocalyptic vision the imagination ever concocted a practical reality. I am therefore not like human beings who were born in earlier centuries. Again I state the obvious, but not without good reason; the impulse to forget this basic fact is strong: who doesn't wish to see himself in the stable frame of ancestors and descendants? I locate myself that way most of the time. It takes a great deal of denial, though, a variety of mental maneuvers and artful refusals of the truth, to go on ignoring the precarity the previous century has created, and the terror, both existential and metaphysical, in which it has steeped me.

By now the epoxy of innocence has been laid on so thick, the propaganda of 1950's and early 1960's pop music and TV is so entrenched, and the sentimentalizing of childhood so pervasive that it might seem to some that I exaggerate when I describe those years as terror, but dread shadowed childhood then. The Cold War wasn't cold for me as a child; it was aflame with a horror actively conjured for me by my teachers, envisioned again and again as a mushroom cloud, a terror refreshed by photos of weapons tests, warnings about godless communism's sole wish to see us all dead, and school- and community-wide air raid drills. I used to lie in my bed at night shaking, near tears, praying the rosary for "world peace," for the Russians to come to their senses and not incinerate us. I dreamt the entire conflagration many times when I was 11 or 12 years old, and the Cuban missile crisis of 1962, when I was 13, made me sick with fear. For years afterward I often woke from a nightmare in which I saw the burning tail of a missile across the sky's canopy reach its apogee and begin its horrifying descent.

In that dream I always tried to ascertain the missile's trajectory, praying that it would land on someone else.

The best people I know are trying, steadfastly, not to succumb to nihilism. With great difficulty they hold fast to an ethical system that poses restraints, that shapes their behavior, that values sacrifice. The great mass of people, by contrast, appear to have defined virtue as obedience to a set of conventions. I used to believe that very nearly everyone possessed at least a modicum of empathy; now most days I feel foolish and wonder where the hell I ever got that notion. I used to believe one could appeal to conscience, or at least to law. But conscience arises from axioms upended entirely in a might-makes -right world. And law, it has become increasingly clear, exists not to ensure fairness but first and foremost to legitimate and protect hierarchic power.

"Have you given up hope/In turning into gold?" Yes. Evidently, many of us have. We continue to set new records for opioid deaths and suicides, and mass shootings. In our shame and despair we have developed an ingenious and largely unconscious disruptive faculty that breaks connections wherever we find them, wherever such connections sneak through the colossal megacomplex of money and noise we call American culture to challenge our delusions.

In a very real way, we are all warriors for the empire; no matter what we think we are doing, no matter what we make. We are inside the largest militarist society the world has ever known, and we are at war always. Trillions of dollars of pensions — teachers', firefighters', nurses' pensions — are tied up in the arms trade. Major universities have hired lobbyists to procure millions in defense contracts. Security is always the stated aim, or technological progress, but the end result is the creation of new markets for weapons. Statecraft involves knowing how to conduct wars that do not spiral out of control, that do not roil the market, that only kill populations with little political power. Appreciation of others, respect for other ways to be human, becomes first a Sunday-school lesson, then something to sneer at, and finally something to rally against to prove we belong with the winners. We live with and export a baseline level of stress the world has seldom known before, and most of it has been normalized by convention. We dare not let down our guard.

The argument is put forth that people need jobs: What people? What jobs? We need teachers; we need builders, farmers, doctors, nurses, plumbers, electricians, firefighters, carpenters, grocers, engineers; we need people to make shoes, boats, pianos, clothing, novels, furniture, music; people to care for the sick and the elderly, to bless us and bury us and repair what's broken.

My next-door neighbor, among the nicest guys I've ever met, is retired from his job as a machinist at General Electric. His house is surrounded by ceramic squirrels and bunnies, gnomes, a birdbath. We talk about the birds, the robin who built a nest in my bicycle helmet, the cardinal with whom he is sure he has a personal relationship (every morning he shells a peanut and leaves it for him.) We talk about our grandkids. His come by on weekends and I hear him chasing them around the yard, "I'm gonna get you! Run! I'm gonna get you!" He catches them and tickles them. He worked at GE for 30 years. I don't know what he was making all those years. Neither does he.

What discourages us from making the connection between a child shot dead in Afghanistan, Syria, or Yemen, and a child shot dead in Newtown, Connecticut, or in Parkland, Florida, or on a playground swing in Boston? Politicians and even gun-control activists seem to believe that the best we can do is modify the technology, the means of killing students and shoppers and concert-goers; they want to reduce the number of bullets — "rounds" — in the magazines of weapons, as if the problem were only that too many people were being killed too fast. The resistance to the carnage largely focuses on the N.R.A., and rightly so; however, the N.R.A. is merely a trade organization like any other, doing all it can to protect its industry. At political debates, or gatherings after the latest episode of crazed killing, people dependably cheer the line, "These are weapons of war and do not belong in our neighborhoods!" What keeps us then from asking whose neighborhood they *do* belong in? Sometimes people say that the AR 15, manufactured exclusively by Colt, is a weapon developed for the "battlefield." As if there were such a thing anymore, as if there were separate militarized areas free of everyone but soldiers who lined up on either side of the field and advanced on a signal like Hussars or Napoleonic infantry. According to creditable sources, civilians account for somewhere between 75 and 90% of deaths in conflict, and more than two thirds of them are children.

The tower will come down, one way or another, the tower of piled weaponry, but before it does, the wars will all have come home; their poisoned waters are already flooding our shores.

The ten-year-old girl shot in the park was named Trina. The park was named for nine-year-old Jermaine, shot there eight years earlier. Of the 27 people gunned down at Sandy Hook Elementary School, 20 were children. Their names have been published along with their photos. Online there is a video taken just moments before the missile struck and roasted the children inside the Yemeni schoolbus, the boys are laughing and throwing a crumpled ball of paper around. And there is a photo of their schoolmates, later, standing by their coffins.

And then there is also, or was, Christopher, eight-years-old, his father standing behind him, hands on his shoulders, proud, as he fired an Uzi at an event held by a Massachusetts Sportsman's Club: "It's all legal & fun — No permits or licenses required!" according to the ad for the event. The fun was to have been shooting at pumpkins, watching their soft flesh splatter, but the Uzi recoiled, jumped in the boy's hands, and in a fraction of a second a bullet entered below his chin and tore through his head.

What maniacal dream unites us? I think back to my cap guns and BB rifle, my heroic silver bullets bringing justice with their delusional righteousness.

Or what about that other neighbor of mine, whose son killed his brother accidentally with a gun his father had not secured? Dear god, that man, whose pain I can barely fathom, whose guilt is forever in his eyes, whom I wish to understand even as I try not to recoil from him: my fellow father, my tragic contemporary, what is his life since then, his post-life life?

Our discourse is poisoned by all that we do not allow ourselves to see about the ways the world has changed, about how it has come under the domination of "le systeme Zaharoff." We are militarist to the max: our rhetoric, our entertainment, our athletic events, our cars, our aesthetics, our very conception of ourselves is congruent with warfare's axioms. More than that, all of nature herself has been compromised by our weapons, our radioactive seawater, our spent uranium, our carcinogenic defoliants. You cannot make modern weapons without mining — iron, bauxite, uranium, lithium — and the required forging of alloys to make death's gleaming toys is a demonic process that surpasses most other industries in poisoning the ecosystem. The resulting cascade of extinctions, could we see it, would look like those films of the glaciers crumbling into the sea. What's more, like arms manufacturing itself, the mining and metals industry is propped up by vast subsidies and a corrupt jiggering of debts, along with bribes, kickbacks, and global systemic corruption.

What will it take to extricate ourselves from this unholy covenant? If we start right now, how many generations? How long before a child on a swing in Boston, a child in a classroom in Connecticut, a child on a schoolbus in Yemen, a child in a hospital in Syria, is safe from the bowling team at Raytheon, the softball team at Colt, the company picnic committee at Northrop Grumman?

What is the future with the present so precarious? We are layers away from any possible clarity, layers of lies from the truth. And so, it could be that this is truly who we are, that it really is our intractable human nature to see strangers as always threatening, as potential aggressors who must be discouraged by our own greater capacity for violence, and to destroy ourselves sorting people into victors and victims. In my lifetime I can find no evidence to the contrary. And yet I cannot allow myself to believe it. I suppose that is the definition of faith — not hope, faith: I have to believe, have often to work to make myself believe, that compromised as we are, we are not cursed, and that although "the sleep is deep and long," we can wake.

HEAD OF A PIN

Every angel is terrifying.

— Rilke

I WAS FREEZING, MY TEETH were chattering and I could not stop shivering. My wife put her hand on my forehead as she brought me another blanket, "You're burning up," she said, and went to get the thermometer: 101.8. "Burning up," yes, but knowing that didn't stop me from experiencing what felt like freezing to death.

I had been fully vaccinated against Covid-19, but I'd read that a small percentage of people contracted the virus even so, and I feared I was one of them. It wasn't my first scare. One year earlier, back in the early days of the pandemic, while we were still spraying the mail with disinfectant, leaving our groceries on the porch until we deemed them safe enough for the fridge and pantry, while we watched in horror as people went into the hospital and died without ever seeing their loved ones again, I spiked a fever. It was April Fool's Day, 2020. I remember that it was raining hard, and I felt sure that on the skylight above my bed I was watching a moonlit private documentary in B&W about my death, a theme running through it that I should have prepared better for this moment.

I was paralyzed with terror. I insisted my wife keep her distance. I was also determined to resist all distractions, any consolations that would require activity: the books on the nightstand, the headphones, the TV, the cupboard, the fridge, as if looking away, even for a moment, would encourage the virus to deliver the *coup de grace*. Once, I would have poured bourbon into a mug in a time like this, but that was 30 years earlier, 33 if it matters.

I kept quiet, unmoving, hoping to hear "the still, small voice" that would counsel me or at least console me. All I heard was borborygmi and a frightened pounding in my ears.

I already knew from experience that a moment would come when I would shake my head and laugh at myself. And that then the laugh would turn bitter. And that, before long, I'd be bawling.

I recognized this heartscape from the time I slept upstairs in my old bedroom above my mother dying on the first floor. And from my stoical calm on a Delta Airlines flight enroute to my younger brother's bedside as he lay dying in the hospital where the two of us were born, that odd laugh escaping just as the plane's tires grabbed the tarmac, the tears arriving as we taxied to the gate.

But that night I still believed there was something especially meant for me in the drumming on the skylight, so I continued listening. Soon, incessant as the rain, question after question came, water on the dark window gleaming as it branched, a miniature river system of fearful uncertainties. Will Kathi be all right? Did I give it to her, too? Will my youngest grandchildren remember me, or are they too young? What use have I been? Is there anything I should do to improve my chances of surviving? How can a creature so small as to be invisible take me down?

The fever broke that night. I didn't have Covid.

But this time, a year later, my doctor's office closed for the weekend, I was directed to Emergency where I received a Covid test. I expected them to treat me and send me home; I was admitted.

My sodium levels had plummeted, my potassium was low, my body continued to burn with fever. What was happening to me? "We don't know," said the Chief Resident, "that's why we're admitting you. Your Covid test was negative."

I was put on a sodium drip, my blood and urine tested frequently. Nurses woke both me and my roommate on the other side of the curtain several times a night to administer a test to one or the other of us. Daytime started with my companion turning on "The 700 Club" at 6 am. I mentioned it to a nurse drawing blood and she said, "Honey, nobody gets any rest in a hospital."

After three days, the Chief Resident came by for a "discharge interview." He pulled up a chair next to my bed and told me my sodium levels had returned to the normal range, my fever had not returned, I seemed alert, and he was sending me home. I had two questions for him. The first — "What happened to me?" — he answered with a shrug, alarming because I hoped to prevent whatever happened from happening again. "Probably a virus, some kind of bug," he sighed. Shrugs and sighs, I've discovered, are a large part of the discourse about viruses.

My second question was a little harder to articulate. I wanted to talk with him about my experience of this illness. I wasn't trying to spin a yarn about it or create an intimacy with him; I was trying to understand what had just happened to me; me, not my blood levels, not my vitals. I said that it felt like I was overcome by a powerful entity that I'd had to struggle against. I said I felt seized by something more powerful than I, taken up, shaken, and put back down after three days. He frowned and looked at his watch. The hospital was filling with patients, several of them probably with Covid19, and he had no time to talk with me. I felt a little guilty for being obtuse about that. I thanked him and he left. But I am still wondering at the strange and powerful encounter I had with the unseen, which reached into dimensions of self, areas of my psyche, that seemed at once fearfully strange and strangely familiar.

The uncanny experience, which recurred several times during my illness, began as a taste. I cannot describe it, I can only say that somehow I was remembering it. I felt as if I were someplace in my emotional landscape, someplace that felt, smelled, and tasted familiar, but I could not connect it to a specific memory. Maybe it was a pre-verbal, infantile memory. As that taste flattened itself into a pervasive dread, adrenaline flushed hot through me, my heart raced, and I felt as if I were falling from a deadly height.

What was terrifying was the feeling that I was not the one doing this remembering but my body, my earthly body, my brain and nervous system, an animal that didn't need some pathetic self hanging around asking dumb questions all the time. It was happening to me, but it had absolutely nothing to do with me. I felt something like déjà vu conjoined with panic. I thought I might be dying, that maybe my body was readying itself for death.

Or maybe it was somehow the taste of entering some next phase of my life, the taste of the gap between this biological moment and the next, something like puberty or menopause, however such transitions are measured, a change I wanted desperately to understand and which, because I could not, produced panic.

The Chief Resident's shrug was just not good enough for me; I had to try to understand what felt like a profound psychic event. Although I often felt I was contending with something implacable, other times I perceived myself caught in the middle of an angry argument between two entities I vaguely remembered, as if I was listening to them from behind a closed door. I couldn't identify them, not quite: both experiences were familar to me from sometime in the past but I could not place them. Maybe they were preverbal memories, if they were memories at all.

Certainly, whatever else it was, it was the argument of my immune system with whatever agent had called it into action. I tried to talk with my doctor about this during my follow-up appointment. Like the hospital physician, he shrugged. But his shrug seemed a gesture of humility. And wonder: 'The body is a continual miracle of self-regulation," he said. I liked his shrug better.

I felt I had been visited by a terrifying angel. I began to describe it to friends as being seized and bound and shaken, hard, before whatever entity had taken me into custody finally let me go. One friend rolled his eyes and said, "Oh Christ, don't go priest on us now!" Another, on the phone, quipped, "Yeah, well, I hear there's a website now where you can order Lourdes water." And I laughed, glad to have such friends.

Don't get me wrong, I am glad, so far as things unseen go, that doctors think more about viruses than angels. And I am even gladder that they admit they know little about the workings of viruses, of the language they speak and the messengers they sometimes are, couriers of tidings that we hardly understand, mysterious companions. We know almost nothing of other orders of being, whether zoonotic or seraphic. I only mean to insist that there is a reality to the felt experience of illness, that it had something to say to me, that it is not merely an inexpert understanding of what's *really* going on.

I hate explanations that shut down wonder, that explain away. I don't think it is a useful definition of the spiritual to consider it what's left over after you have snuffed out each of the candles you can reach with an explanation.

What we experience is shaped by our imagination, where encounters with unseen forces are interpreted, in personal terms, in one mode of language or another. The imagination is a vast realm where myth and music, stories and visions, hold sway. Our lives are always interpretations. Consciousness is a profoundly metaphorical drama staged by the imagination. This is how I understand these lines by William Carlos Williams, himself a physician, who wrote in "Asphodel, That Greeny Flower."

> Only the imagination is real!
> I have declared it.
> Time without end.

In Catholic school, in first grade, we were often reminded by our teacher, Sister Anne Catherine, that we should skootch over and leave half the sculpted wooden seat for our guardian angel. We all obeyed. Not one of us smirked. And I am not smirking now. I happen to think it is a beautiful idea; it was a real comfort to me, a wise, reassuring, and generous gift given to a nervous child. Each of us had our own Guardian Angel, she told us, who knew us long before we were born. I tried to turn my head quick to maybe surprise my angel, to see him. Once I even had myself convinced I'd caught a glimpse, just a movement and a light, out of the corner of my eye. And so, when I explore the experience of being ill, I find there's an angel there, an elusive being born in my imagination as a Catholic child.

But it isn't necessary to embrace the cartoon angels offered to six year olds, any more than it is required to believe a virus is "some kind of bug." It is possible (I am doing it now) to reach into the unseen with questions and a wondering imagination, and to follow our intuition, knowing that we are in relation to much that is unseen and unknown but nevertheless important.

I was discharged the day before my 72nd birthday. The next day I woke early, and whether by simple contrast to my illness or because I'd returned home to sleep in my own bed, I felt better than I had in years.

Fifteen years earlier I had been diagnosed with a condition called *Essential Thrombocythemia*, a disorder of the bone marrow that produces too many platelets, the blood's clotting material. It is a blood cancer, often a precursor to leukemia, but it is not itself a mortal danger. It puts those afflicted at higher risk for vascular blockages and stroke, and in my case it slows me down. "I wake to sleep and take my waking slow," as Theodore Roethke wrote. It has always taken me half the day to come fully to consciousness, and some days I'm not sure I ever get there. I have thought — secretly of course but I'll confess it, sheepishly, here, that it is because I am a genius; I have so much to gather up, from so many different provinces of self, so many dimensions of the mind, that of course it takes me a long time each day to reintegrate the many parts of me and bring them to bear on the day's obligations! But the more likely explanation is that the thrombocythemic thickening of my blood means my poor heart is pumping syrup, so it takes a long time to get up to speed. The experience of that torpor is sometimes a delicious languor, other times a maddening frustration. Treatment for *Thrombocythemia* includes carefully monitoring platelet levels in the blood; mine were consistently an alarming 500 or so points above the normal range.

In addition, microscopy showed that in addition to an overabundance of platelets, I had somehow incurred a mutation called Janus 2. As the doctor explained to me that a normal platelet is designed to adhere to others by means of spicules radiating from one side of it, and that mine had suffered a mutation that resulted in spicules jutting from two sides of the platelet, I understood immediately, or was at least able to envision that platelet as Janus, the two-faced god of doorways. I remember that I quipped, "No wonder I don't know whether I'm coming or going." The doctor looked at me blankly; he didn't know who Janus was.

Two days after my hospitalization I received the discharge report, which included a full battery of blood tests: my platelet count was inexplicably back in the normal range. Excited, I called my doctor who could only say that sometimes cancers do go into spontaneous remission. "Each of us have our own immune system," he said. Again he marveled at the body's wisdom, the ability of an individual's immune system to restore one to health. "Let's hope it lasts," he said, "Let's continue the three month labs and we'll keep an eye on things." I felt great: lighter, more energetic, mentally clearer, and grateful to whatever had taken hold of me, "burning me up" and sending me to the ER, grateful to the doctors in the hospital, grateful to whatever entity — my immune system, my guardian angel, had somehow left me healthier than I'd been in years.

Of course I am aware that this is just what an old man needs, especially in the very month he is retiring: the illusion of renewal, of a fresh start, whether granted by metaphysical or microbial beings. And it was spring! Even so, does that invalidate the experience of renewal? We are back to the question of language, of metaphor, of how we think and feel about events; in a phrase, "what we make of them."

If you remove subjectivity from the calculus, if you exorcise the imagination and enshrine the remainder as truth, you're left with the kind of data-driven discourse that starts with what happened last time, and tries, via statistics and probability, to determine what we might reasonably expect next time — the statistician as haruspex, the result sufficient unto itself. But when we want to talk about what we ourselves have experienced, we resort, time and again, to metaphor. Metaphor is the language of spirit.

So I am still here with the question: What happened to me? Sodium crashed, potassium deficient, body burnt up with fever — was this the result of a lapse in the immune system's protection, allowing an invader to enter?

We still talk in militarist terms about it; the immune system is said to "fight germs," meaning harmful bacteria. But we have come to find that other bacteria are essential to our well-being. The same is likely true of viruses. The immune system is immeasurably complex. It doesn't just repel invaders like some 80's video game, it attempts to repair disruption and disequilibrium. It may be that some viruses are the allies that the immune system calls upon for help.

I realize that with Covid-19 still claiming millions of lives around the world, it may not be the best time to explore the salutary potential of viruses. ("Jeez, read the room, man!") But still. The angel of death is not the only angel.

We live on a *Planet of Viruses,* which is the title of science writer Carl Zimmer's survey discussing our evolving knowledge of the virosphere. "It is estimated that there are 10^{31} virus particles in the oceans," he writes," — they vastly outnumber all other organisms on the planet." A single cubic inch contains billions of viruses.

According to Zimmer, the word virus is Latin for both venom and semen. Of course it is the few deadly viruses that get our attention, but the vast numbers of viruses that we encounter do not affect us, or do so in ways we're largely unaware of. But that venom/semen paradox is not even the most bedeviling one: there is ongoing disagreement about whether viruses are alive at all, whether they are living beings or tiny specks of dead matter.

It's hard not to feel that we are entering the realm of philosophy or even theology here, having to ask, ultimately, what we mean when we say the words "living" and "dead," and entertaining the idea that the virosphere may be the true ground of our being, the eternal potential from which life springs, differentiates, changes. If we were swimming in a water drop, the water would be made of viruses.

The position that viruses cannot be said to be alive rests in part on their absence from taxonomy: they are not Eukaryota, not Bacteria, not Archaea. If Taxonomy charts were maps, viruses would require a *Here Be Dragons* inscription. Evolutionary biologist Luis P. Villareal, writing in *Scientific American*, complains that "The categorization of viruses as nonliving during much of the modern era of biological science has had an unintended consequence: it has led most researchers to ignore viruses in the study of evolution."

It is likely that life began some 4 billion years ago with these bits of genetic information, instructions for building protein molecules. It is hard to think of time as time when it is conceived on that scale, and it is hard then not to see viruses as agents of eternity, present everywhere always, coming and going in our very cells, occasionally surfacing in our human reality.

It turns out that there are some viruses that behave so much like our own bodies' cells that they can also be infected by viruses. These smaller viruses, called virophages or simply 'phages' can alter the genome of the viruses they invade. This discovery has led to a revolution in medical research, and that research has, in large part, led most recently to the discovery of a vaccine for Covid 19.

Viruses, it seems, are so ubiquitous they are a kind of global haze of unused genetic information, a kind of pervasive cloud of genetic particulate like ash or dust. (That taste in my mouth, was it ashes?) This dead genetic material is operative everywhere as legacy, curse, influence. It might be said that viruses are pure potential, an entire universe of possibilities, the eternal from which time flickers and flares.

So, are viruses therefore life un-coalesced? Letters in a vast and mostly undiscovered alphabet? Ideas unarticulated? Genetic engineers? Evolutionary biologists have suggested that viruses are the link between current living things, which continue via the replication of their DNA, to a prior realm of creatures based on RNA. What does this mean? About time? About life? The future? Evolution? Our place in the welter of Ovidian metamorphoses? Are viruses our distant ancestors?

Or are they angels? I was seized and taken from my life and shaken.

While virology is a science in its infancy, the study of angels has been avidly pursued for millennia. Getting the jump on a metaphor that evolutionary biologists have applied to viruses, Augustine, in the 5th century, asserted that we are in the soil of God's garden, and the angels are the gardeners that tend us. "It is easier to know what they do than what they are," he wrote, which might well be the complaint of a contemporary virologist.

It turns out that what viruses do is enter our cells and use their reproductive apparatus to make copies of themselves, in the process switching on or off certain genes, and otherwise changing our DNA. So, even leaving God out of the equation (since that three-letter word is too fraught, too compromised, too imprecise and corrupted) they can be said to be gardening us, and over eons modifying our physiology and changing our destiny, speaking directly to our bodies, caught up in relentless metamorphoses across innumerable generations.

What our senses cannot perceive, we know with our imaginations. We are hybrid creatures. We don't simply live in the biosphere. Life is biological, living it is imaginary. Although I can watch raindrops coursing and ramifying, hesitating, essaying, on a moonlit skylight, I cannot for the life of me imagine a way to argue with, plead with, or dissuade such an infinitesimal entity as a virus. Believe me, I tried.

While writing this essay, I received a golden angel medallion in the mail with a request for money to support the work of Catholic relief services. The image stamped on either side is identical: a robed figure, winged, with folded, praying hands, as if Janus himself was an angel. It would make a great coin for rigged betting: call "heads" and you could never lose. It brought out every hard-earned cynical response I ever had to the Catholic Church as an institution, that global real estate empire disguised as an instrument of God, that to my mind — and history I believe bears me out — is clearly a pathogen. At the same time, if a person is thus moved to send money and if (a big if) the money actually helps someone in need, then has the respondent somehow made the angel real? It appears that, like viruses, angels have no way to reproduce other than by entering into a host: in this case the human imagination. Perhaps what wings represent is the ability — the necessity? — to fly back and forth between these twin realities?

I hope it is obvious that I am not arguing for a retreat into angelogy (no Lourdes water for me, thanks.) I only mean to point to a rich reservoir of metaphor and insist that our forbears were not all benighted, superstitious dolts. Our ancestors were imaginative artists who tried to understand what was happening to them. We think in metaphors, explicit or implied, interacting with those metaphors in story, parable, allegory. At the same time, all our conceptualizing, our art, our language itself, seen against the vastness of cosmological time and the constancy of the virosphere, is only something that's been thrown together in a moment, a put-up job, a blurted reply to the questions and requirements of the world. Odds are we are much more likely on any occasion to be wrong than right and certainly unlikely to ever find our way to a comprehensive understanding of life, whether by scientific or metaphysical inquiry. Our autobiographies, no matter how detailed, are a mere epithelium. Everything, including ourselves, is more complex and mysterious than we can comprehend. Electron microscopes peer into inner space and photograph viruses that are orders of magnitude smaller than even bacteria. One of those viruses has killed nearly five million people around the world and is even now killing about 10,000 people every day — clearly real, an agent of fate, no matter how tiny. According to Dionysus the Areopagite, living in 1st century Greece, the Athenians always raised, in addition to their other altars, an altar to "an unknown god," which seems to me an admirable gesture of humility.

A few months after my illness, my platelet count began to rise again. I was disappointed of course, but it had taken decades to climb to the alarming number that signaled *Thrombocythemia*, more decades than I probably have left anyway. I'm not worried about it, and I am grateful for the chance to be a foolish, hopeful, curious old man overtaken by wonder and a thirst for miracles.

Or maybe I was only moving from station to station along the interior walls of my hopelessly Catholic post-Catholic skull. Maybe I was trying to prepare for my death. The same friend who'd begged me not to "go priest on us" told me, "Old guys always get philosophical when they get sick." It was such a gentle verbal poke in the ribs, that all at once I remembered why I love him.

We are surrounded by invisible companions, in a timeless conversation, as centuries of angelogy insist. Virology describes this conversation: RNA changing DNA or modifying it, activating and deactivating certain genes. The immune system is an individualized genetic organization that extends backward into evolutionary time: bespoke, unique, transcending history but also made of it. It is there to be relied on for protection without our having to ask for it, there from time immemorial, a memory of eternity, an emanation of health, a measure to determine what ought to be. An angel by any other name would be as sweet. However we conceive of them, it is for both viruses and angels to *do*, to cause, to effect change and shape destiny. We who are their foes and fools and wombs must wonder. That's how we are made; that's what we're for — to wonder. We want to know what is happening to us.

SEABIRDS

"... if you look at walls covered with many stains ... with the idea of imagining some scene, you will see in it a similarity to landscapes adorned with mountains, rivers, rocks, trees, plains, broad valleys, and hills of all kinds. You may also see in it battles and figures with lively gestures and strange faces and costumes and an infinity of things which you can reduce to separate and complex forms. And with these walls ... it is as with the sound of bells; in their ringing you may find all the sounds and words that you wish to imagine."

— Leonardo da Vinci, 1492

I WAS EIGHTEEN WHEN I FIRST saw the ocean. I stood on the boardwalk in Ocean City New Jersey and nodded at the Atlantic. It looked as I'd imagined. The boardwalk smelled of suntan lotion and french-fries.

Three years later, as a college student, I signed on to an oceanographic research voyage as a summer job. We spent two weeks off The Grand Banks before heading for Iceland where I was too sick to get off the ship. I never really got my sea legs. When I wasn't ill, I was queasy with the fumes from the ship's engines. The U.S.S. Josiah Willard Gibbs was a converted seaplane tender, not a large craft, with a lab aboard, run jointly by Bell Labs and the U.S. Navy. The research had to do with underwater sound.

My badge said I was a "Navigator," which only meant that, below decks, I sat in front of a Loran-C machine that displayed the ship's coordinates. The entire expanse of the ocean is a machine-read electronic grid. Every 15 minutes, I would check our Loran-C against our last position on a chart that showed our planned course as a blue line. If we were off, I'd use a compass and protractor to measure how far, and radio the bridge. Simple, boring, smelly with fumes.

I have two distinct memories from those weeks at sea. The first is a storm that brought waves of twenty-five to thirty feet, which feels like being in an elevator going up two floors and then down two floors and then up two floors, over and over. My stomach remembers that one. The other was a clear night of stars that helped me understand the word "firmament" — more stars than the spaces between them, the sky something firm, not mere space, and much more substantial than the day's pellucid cerulean.

I'd brought only one book with me, *Hamlet's Mill* by Giorgio de Santillana and Hertha von Dechend, a dense hardcover tome with a beautiful image on its cover: a great tree, *axis mundi*, breaking through the crust of earth's orb and branching to connect a scattering of stars.

I had been reading Jung since my Psychology class the previous semester, and one evening, around a hookah, stoned with friends on a braided rug, I began enthusing about the collective unconscious, especially about all the instances of syncretic myths and tales across cultures and continents. It seemed so promising to me — to think that we possess one species-large consciousness! I was after all at a Catholic University, steeped in the idea of a "body of Christ of which we are the members," and more than a little desperate for evidence that the war-torn and apocalyptic world of 1969 could be somehow understood. One of the circle — who I remember well and gratefully, but not, sadly, his name — interrupted me. He protested that there was no need to come up with such a quasi-religious explanation: "We're all looking at the same sky, man. Those are sailors' stories. They're about stars and planets and weather and water, man." Then he put the hose to his mouth, burbled a hit, and passed it to the person next to him. "Hamlet's Mill!" he said, exhaling smoke. "That's the book to read. That book is out of sight, man."

Aboard ship I read and reread the book when I was not on watch. I couldn't entirely follow its convoluted argument; I kept being hijacked by my enthusiasm for some myth or another from one place or another on the globe. Still, my stoned friend was pretty much on the money: the myths we know, according to the authors, are the tales of seafarers, merchants essential to the development of cities, and were meant to communicate astronomical observations in narrative form for navigational and geo-positioning purposes. I remember standing at the rail, awed not only by the sweep of the milky way, but also by the brilliance of those long gone artist-astronomers. I spent a long time above decks that night. As the waves picked up, I watched the flying fish, schools of them, leaping from wave to wave. Later, the Bosun explained to me that they only appear to fly; that they swim in a straight line just under the surface, the movement of the waves exposing them at intervals.

When I moved here, to Salem, Massachusetts, a historic seaport, I was 68 years old, and the soggy wet bottom of the country had just given way. Donald Trump had become the 45th president of the United States. Just around that time I read somewhere that Thoreau said he loved the Atlantic shore because there all of America was behind him. That seemed about right to me even then, back when we thought America could not be more outrageous, cruel, and violent, back before we had ever heard of Covid-19 or had to endure the stupidity and callousness and selfishness of our leaders while nearly 400,000 of us died.

I moped around for the whole first year. I had to drive into Boston three days a week to teach, and driving back to Salem always made me sad: I had lived in Cambridge thirty years and I missed my life. I had the good sense to complain to a friend that I was low. She had grown up in Salem. "You need to develop a relationship to the water," she said. Perhaps it was a failure of the imagination, but I decided I should therefore buy a boat.

When I shared this with my wife, her ancient, aboriginal, ancestral sigh left no doubt what she thought of the idea. But it turned out that friends of ours had a little wooden skiff they'd built themselves, a beautiful twelve footer, for sale, with a 5hp Mercury outboard, complete with trailer. They delivered it to the backyard where it sat for a good while until one day I decided, damn it, now or never, and with a new Salem friend, also a writer, I trailered the boat to the launch. It took, I think, seventeen attempts to back the trailer down the ramp and into the water. At one point I jacknifed completely into an L: I looked from my driver's window and there, beside me, was my boat! By the time I succeeded, an amused crowd of mariners, including the harbormaster and the Coast Guard crew, had gathered, shaking their heads.

I took the boat out on the water a total of four times that summer, enough to learn that it was too small. Two adults would have it riding so low in the water that if you gripped the gunwale your fingers would skim the surface. It felt like sitting on a sheet of plywood on the ocean. And even boats that were trying to be careful could capsize us if I didn't remain alert and steer — *wump, wump, wump* — directly across the wake while gunning the engine. Since then, the boat rests on its trailer in the yard, covered completely in a sagging tarp that has filled with rainwater and become an extremely popular birdbath. Starlings, sparrows, jays, mourning doves, and cardinals gather in my neighbor's scraggly tree or bounce on long wands of forsythia, making a racket while they wait their turn.

These days I walk or ride my bike half a mile to Salem Willows Park. The water on my left, Collins Cove, opens into the broader harbor just beyond Dead Horse Beach. I've heard the story of that funky name in several versions: that a dead horse was found there, washed ashore and stinking. Or that it was the site of a burial ground for farm animals. Or my favorite, that this was the place appointed for bringing dead horses, some peculiarity of the tides here perfect for gathering up those offerings and carrying them out through the harbor, past the islands, into the open sea. I can't vouch for that version however. But I like it too much not to let it be.

Soon there are grassy areas and picnic tables, The Clam Shack, the ancient willows (and oaks and sycamores) that the park is named for, a honky-tonk strip of take-out restaurants:

pizza, Chinese food, soft-serve ice cream, and the best popcorn in the world turned in a giant metal drum, old-school, at E. W. Hobbs, served in red and white striped boxes. I continue on, park my bike, sit on a bench, and watch lobster boats, motorboats and sailboats, making their way into or out of the harbor. And the Boston Ferry. And the schooner, *Fame*, out of Pickering Wharf. It reminds me of the west coast of Ireland. My favorite spot juts out into the harbor, as far as you can go on land. There are three benches there, each with a dedicatory plaque:

Edward & Dolores Zielinski
Champions For
Family, Salem & the Willows
Best Parents & Best Popcorn

What a story unfolds from this one! You can sit down and look out past the Misery Islands into a fog just beginning to roll into the harbor and wonder at three generations of Zielinskis: that last line tells me that the donors of this bench were, while strictly speaking anonymous, Edward and Dolores's children, and I can think of only one explanation for "Best Popcorn" and that would involve a young grandchild, equally anonymous: "And what do you remember best about Babka and Gigi?"

And what about:

Teddy & Gina Jaworski
Always Reminiscing and Wishing
Married In Italy, September 26 1948

Reminiscing about what? Wishing for what? Or shall we read that as "remembering Italy and wishing we were back there?" I hear a sigh in the way it's phrased. Can we infer that Teddy (Tadeusz?) was an Allied soldier stationed in post-WWII Italy? Gina a war orphan? A martyred Partisan's daughter? A hanged Fascista's? I'm stretching, I know, but the past is foggy, made of distance and plausibility. There are dead horses in it, I think, and immigrants' dreams, and sailors telling stories about the stars, and shipwrecks. And Italy. And untold other things to reminisce about or wish for.

Even the simplest and most conventional of the three:

In Loving Memory of
Carol A. Giberti

offers much more to read than the words. I find myself staring at it, while questions swell and break one after the other, engendered, it seems, by the water and salt air. This mental state, a reorientation, a re-minding that happens, is a kind of ionization of the imagination; soon things take on significance, one way or another: metaphorical, allegorical, associational, consequential. It may be just a brackish whiff of what those earliest seafarers experienced under the strewn and clustered stars.

The pandemic arrived in March, and everything shut down. Then, as spring eased into summer, the take-out joints at The Willows sometimes opened for a few hours of the day. I stood, masked, in the socially distanced line to E.W. Hobbs, but now I think that whether we knew it or not at the time, we were all less interested in popcorn than in reinforcing the idea that the pandemic was merely an inconvenience.

I needed something to occupy my mind on my walks besides the dread of the pandemic, so I started taking pictures. I didn't usually remember to check the tide chart, having no practical reason to do so; I just showed up to see what was going on.

With a camera around my neck, or even only taking photos with my phone (a little bit of etymological synesthesia, that) whatever faces me speaks only the language of light. The water changes all day long. One moment it's a dull nickel, the next a reticulated, wobbling web of light. The sky is similarly inconstant; weather changes in a moment here. More than once I dressed for the bright blue day out my window to find that the day had turned gray in the time it took me to change from my pandemic pj's to a pair of pants. Last winter, storms mangled the pier, twisting its pilings and splintering several planks of the wooden deck my grandson and I had rumbled over so many times on our bikes. I took some photos of that. No fishing from there till the city engineers have made repairs. It looks like the whole thing will need to be rebuilt.

Like so much else now.

Photography sufficed for a while, but to look at the photos on my phone was not very different from zoom really, more flat images on a glass screen, and I was tired of zoom, tired of screens, tired of better-than-nothing. If I were a real photographer, I might find that the camera was helping me pay attention, keeping me alert to things I might photograph. I have heard photographers say that, and I'd wanted it to be so, but I'm someone who doesn't even like wearing my glasses outside; they make me feel, I don't know, indoors, as if I'm looking through a window, and looking through a camera only seems to remove me further, to make me feel even less present.

I had wanted to bring the outside inside. I wanted to bring the water, the rocks, the waves, the sky, the trees, the light, inside, home, but my photos never captured the movement of the waves — the way they take the light, the sounds they make slapping the slick green pylons of the pier, raking the pebbles from Dead Horse Beach, sometimes loudly sucking and slurping at a cluster of rocks — let alone the moods stirred in me. Taking pictures got me out of the house and down to the water, but it wasn't very satisfying.

At least, not until I started taking photos in order to paint them. I'd shoot the sea, the horizon, the wrack line, the reeds, the rocks, fog, clouds, gulls and bring them back like a fisherman's daily catch. Then I'd paint, in watercolors, with the photo as my prompt. I felt as if I was making them somehow three-dimensional again. I struggled with the medium, which, for me as a beginner and amateur, is balky but becomes, as I paint, a deeper encounter than the photo; sometimes for a moment even deeper than having been there. I paint by light I remember, and I try to depict it, along with its shadows and patches of cool shade and messages about time and weather, not quite as it is in the photograph, but as I remember it, with its smells and breezes and loud gulls fighting over popcorn. Strictly speaking, a painting is also two dimensional, but not for the painter, not really. And in the case of seascapes, if they're successful, there is a bit of trickery in them, a mild *tromp l'oeil*, that communicates distance; the experience of depth and height is the point, mostly.

When I was much younger, I tried my hand at oil painting. Watercolors are different; they're, well, *water.* They obey gravity. They can be inter-absorbent, transparent, or opaque, like people. They are less willing to be merely used, less compliant with the artist's intention: they drip, pool, run, evaporate, and invite not so much mastery or virtuosity, as dialogue.

Watercolor, it turns out, is my relationship to the water.

Sometimes, with or without a photo to prompt me, I start by drawing a line and staring at it until I see it as a horizon. Then I put something simple below the line — a post, a tree, a boxy little house, anything, just to establish a perspective, to add dimension to the flatness, to suggest a matrix on which other objects are to be distributed. But it is important to paint, not merely draw and color it in. As a landscape or seascape emerges from the paper, I sometimes see that it comes close to a real place that I know, that memory serves up, and I put in one or two more details that would suggest the place to anyone who has been there.

Once, when I had used a light card stock, not watercolor paper, the supersaturated paper left behind a few specks of erupted pulp when it dried, darkened raised crumbs, as if from an eraser. They were in the area just above the horizon and seemed, to me, configured as distant seabirds wheeling in fog. I reached for a pencil to trace them, maybe to claim them, to insist on them, but it was time to step away. It's important to know when to step away.

ACKNOWLEDGMENTS

I want to thank the editors of the following journals, online magazines, and blogs where these essays first appeared, sometimes in slightly different form: *The Woven Tale Press, Brevity, River Teeth, Janus Head, Plume, The Tahoma Literary Review, Solstice, Post Road, Flashpoint, Agni, Talking Writing, Consequence,* and *Chautauqua.*

Special thanks to Kathleen Aguero, Dewitt Henry, Lee Hope, Joe Mackall, Tom Mallouk, Caitlin McGill, Frederick Reiken, Mimi Schwartz, J.D. Scrimgeour, Baron Wormser, and Mako Yoshikawa for their collegial assistance with these essays and for their writerly friendship and support.

I'm deeply grateful to Steve Harvey, The Humble Essayist himself, for suggesting this book, and for his editorial guidance, especially regarding what to include or leave out in a collection that represents half a century of writing.

Richard Hoffman is the author of seven books, including the memoirs *Half the House* and *Love & Fury*. He has published four books of poetry: *Without Paradise; Gold Star Road,* winner of The Barrow Street Press Poetry Prize and the Sheila Motton Book Award from The New England Poetry Club; *Emblem*; and *Noon until Night,* which received the 2018 Massachusetts Book Award for Poetry; as well as the story collection, *Interference and Other Stories*. He is Emeritus Writer in Residence at Emerson College and Nonfiction Editor of *Solstice: A Magazine of Diverse Voices*.

REMEMBERING THE ALCHEMISTS
& Other Essays

Designed by Richard Skinner
(delanoir2@gmail.com)
Typeset in Calisto MT

www.ingramcontent.com/pod-product-compliance
Lightning Source LLC
Chambersburg PA
CBHW051144190726
48290CB00006B/1987

* 9 7 8 1 7 3 4 5 1 7 7 6 7 *